AbleMUSE
A REVIEW OF POETRY, PROSE & ART

NUMBER 20
Winter 2015

www.ablemuse.com

Able Muse Press
publishing the new, the established

Now available from Able Muse Press:

Able Muse Anthology
Edited by Alexander Pepple
Foreword by Timothy Steele

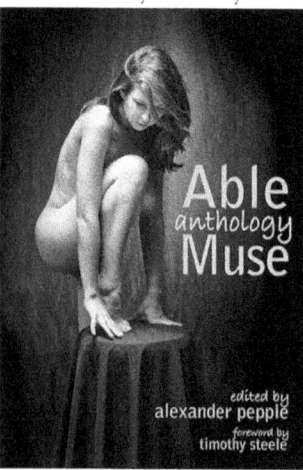

978-0-9865338-0-8 • $16.95

With R.S. Gwynn, Rhina P. Espaillat, Rachel Hadas, Mark Jarman, Timothy Murphy, Dick Davis, A.E. Stallings, Alan Sullivan, Deborah Warren, Diane Thiel, Leslie Monsour, Kevin Durkin, Turner Cassity, Kim Bridgford, Richard Moore and others.

". . . Here's a generous serving of the cream of Able Muse including not only formal verse but nonmetrical work that also displays careful craft, memorable fiction (seven remarkable stories), striking artwork and photography, and incisive prose." — X.J. Kennedy

Able Muse – Inaugural Print Edition

WITH:

POEMS, FICTION, BOOK REVIEWS, INTERVIEWS & ESSAYS from catherine tufariello • catharine savage brosman • leslie monsour • ned balbo • ted mc carthy • diane seuss • susan mclean • rebecca foust • j. patrick lewis • john slater • gail white • kim bridgford • nancy lou canyon • john whitworth • peter filkins • marilyn l. taylor • and others

ISBN 978-0-9865338-2-2

Subscribe to: *Able Muse (Print Ed.)*

Semiannual review of poetry, prose & art

Able Muse (Print Edition) continues the excellence in poetry, art, fiction, essays, interviews and book reviews showcased all these years in the online edition. Subscribe at *www.ablemusepress.com*

For complete details, visit: **www.AbleMusePress.com**

visit

Able Muse

online for more than a decade of archives, plus web-only features not available in the Print Edition at:

www.ablemuse.com

Able Muse is not just another poetry site. It is one of the best sites on the Internet.
—Heather O'Neil, *Suite101.com*

Eratosphere

A forum of Able Muse Review

Able Muse's premier online forums and workshops for metrical and non-metrical poetry, fiction, translations, art, nonfiction and discussions at:

http://eratosphere.ablemuse.com

Able Muse and its extraordinary companion website, the ***Eratosphere,*** have created a huge and influential virtual literary community. —Dana Gioia

Able Muse
www.ablemuse.com

Editor	Alexander Pepple
Assistant Poetry Editors	Stephen Kampa, Richard Meyer, Callie Siskel
Nonfiction Editor	Gregory Dowling
Fiction Editor	Karen Kevorkian
Assistant Fiction Editors	Jonathan Danielson, Janice D. Soderling, Rob Wright
Editorial Board	Rachel Hadas, X.J. Kennedy, A.E. Stallings, Timothy Steele, Deborah Warren

Able Muse is published semiannually. Subscription rates—for individuals: $24.00 per year; libraries and institutions: $34 per year; single and previous issues: $16.95 + $3 S&H. International subscription rates: $33 per year; single and previous issues: $16.95 + $5 S&H. Subscribe online at www.ablemusepress.com or send a check payable to *Able Muse Review* to the snail mail address indicated below. (USD throughout. Online payment with WePay/credit card.)

We read year-round and welcome previously unpublished manuscripts only. No simultaneous submissions. Online or email submissions ONLY. Submission guidelines available at: www.ablemuse.com/submit

Queries and other correspondence should be emailed to: editor@ablemuse.com
For paper correspondence, be sure to include a self-addressed, stamped envelope:

Attn: Alexander Pepple, Editor
Able Muse Review
467 Saratoga Avenue #602
San Jose, CA 95129

Library of Congress Control Number: 2015955765

ISBN 978-1-927409-63-3 (paperback) / ISBN 978-1-927409-64-0 (digital)

ISSN 2168-0426

Cover images: "Audience" by Patrick McDonald
Cover & book design by Alexander Pepple

www.ablemuse.com
editor@ablemuse.com

Printed in the United States of America
Published in 2015 by Able Muse Press: www.ablemusepress.com

Alexander Pepple

Editorial

In this issue, Amit Majmudar, who has appeared in these pages several times in the past, is our featured poet. He speaks with Daniel Brown in an enlightening and sometimes provocative interview. Our showcased artist Léon Leijdekkers brings us his striking black-and-white photographs of places.

Included are our usual complement of new poetry, poetry translations, fiction, essays, interviews, and book reviews from contributors X.J. Kennedy, Kim Bridgford, Catharine Savage Brosman, Wendy Videlock, Beth Houston, Dan Campion, Peter Kline, Lynda Sexson, Paul Soto, N.S. Thompson, Moira Egan, Robert B. Shaw, Stephen Kampa, and others.

We present in this issue the winners and finalists of the fifth annual *Able Muse* contests: for the 2015 Able Muse Write Prize, congratulations to Elise Hempel (for poetry, as selected by final judge H.L. Hix) and Andrea Witzke Slot (for fiction, as selected by final judge Eugenia Kim). Kudos also goes to the finalists whose work is represented here: Jeanne Wagner and, again, Elise Hempel.

We also congratulate Emily Leithauser for *The Borrowed World,* winner of the 2015 Able Muse Book Award as selected by final judge Peter Campion. Some of our finalists will, likewise, receive a standard Able Muse Press publication contract. A special thank you to the accomplished poets and writers who participated in our blind reading and shortlisting in the early judging stages.

We have made six nominations for the 2016 Pushcart Prize. These include two poems from the previous issue ("How can I" by Eric McHenry and "Correcting Frame" by Maura Stanton); two poems from the current issue ("Xenia" by Ryan Wilson and "Shopping with Whitney Houston" by Autumn Newman); and two stories from the previous issue ("A Journey from Which Many Do Not Return" by Linda Boroff and "Action Figures" by Lane Kareska).

Moving along, I am pleased to announce that we are now open for submissions to the 2016 run of *Able Muse* contests. We are honored to have three illustrious final judges: Patricia Smith for the Write Prize for Poetry, Stuart Dybek for the Write Prize for Fiction;

and A.E. Stallings for the Able Muse Book Award. Entry deadlines are provided in these pages, and details at the Able Muse Press website, www.ablemusepress.com.

Submissions are open year-round for our regular issues, per the guidelines available online at www.ablemuse.com/submit/.

Able Muse Press has been busy with the release of a new short story collection, *Times Square and Other Stories* by William Baer; and new books of poetry, including *Slingshots and Love Plums,* the third full-length collection from Wendy Videlock; *Taking Shape,* a full-length collection of carmina figurata by Jan D. Hodge. We also have releases from the 2014 Able Muse Book Award: *Asperity Street,* the full-length collection from special honoree Gail White; and the winning collection *Cause for Concern* by Carrie Shipers.

We welcome our new assistant editor Richard Meyer for poetry. We offer thanks to our departing assistant editor (Reagan Upshaw for poetry), as well as to our returning editors (Karen Kevorkian, fiction, and Gregory Dowling, nonfiction), and assistant editors (Jonathan Danielson, Janice D. Soderling and Rob Wright, fiction, and Stephen Kampa, and Callie Siskel, poetry).

We appreciate your continued support of *Able Muse* and Able Muse Press, and hope you'll enjoy this issue as much as we've enjoyed bringing it to you.

The very best,

Alexander Pepple
—Editor

BOOKS
FROM
ABLE MUSE PRESS

NEW & RECENT RELEASES

Carrie Shipers: Cause for Concern – Poems
~ Winner, 2015 Able Muse Book Award ~

Gail White: Asperity Street – Poems
~ Special Honoree, 2014 Able Muse Book Award ~

Melissa Balmain: Walking in on People – Poems
~ Winner, 2013 Able Muse Book Award ~

Jeredith Merrin: Cup – Poems
~ Special Honoree, 2013 Able Muse Book Award ~

Chelsea Woodard: Vellum – Poems

D.R. Goodman: Greed: A Confession – Poems

Richard Newman: All the Wasted Beauty of the World – Poems

Ellen Kaufman: House Music – Poems

Barbara Ellen Sorensen: Compositions of the Dead Playing Flutes – Poems

Frank Osen: Virtue, Big as Sin – Poems
~ Winner, 2012 Able Muse Book Award ~

James Pollock: Sailing to Babylon – Poems

Matthew Buckley Smith: Dirge for an Imaginary World – Poems
~ Winner, 2011 Able Muse Book Award ~

April Lindner: This Bed Our Bodies Shaped – Poems

Richard Wakefield: A Vertical Mile – Poems

William Baer: Times Square and Other Stories

Jan D. Hodge: Taking Shape – Carmina Figurata

Hollis Seamon: Corporeality – Stories

Wendy Videlock: Slingshots and Love Plums – Poems

Martin McGovern: Bad Fame – Poems

William Conelly: Uncontested Grounds – Poems

John Philip Drury: Sea Level Rising – Poems

Carol Light: Heaven from Steam – Poems

Stephen Scaer: Pumpkin Chucking – Poems

Maryann Corbett: Credo for the Checkout Line in Winter – Poems

Wendy Videlock: The Dark Gnu and Other Poems

Ben Berman: Strange Borderlands – Poems

Catherine Chandler: Lines of Flight – Poems

Margaret Ann Griffiths: Grasshopper: The Poetry of M A Griffiths

Wendy Videlock: Nevertheless – Poems

Aaron Poochigian: The Cosmic Purr – Poems

Michael Cantor: Life in the Second Circle – Poems

LATEST ABLE MUSE PRESS CATALOG

Free Download at: www.ablemusepress.com/catalog

2016 Able Muse Write Prize
for *poetry & fiction*

» **$500 prize** *for the poetry winner*
   » *All poetry styles welcome (metrical & free verse)*

» **$500 prize** *for the fiction winner*

» *plus,* **publication** *in Able Muse (Print Edition)*

» ***Blind judging*** *by the final judges*

» ***Final Judges***: *Patricia Smith (poetry);*
         Stuart Dybek (fiction)

» ***Entry Deadline:*** *March 15, 2016*

**GUIDELINES & ENTRY INFORMATION
AVAILABLE ONLINE AT:**
www.ablemusepress.com

ABLE MUSE BOOK PRIZE

2016 Able Muse Book Award
for poetry

» ***$1000 prize*** *for winning manuscript, plus*

» ***publication*** *by Able Muse Press*

» *All poetry styles welcome (metrical & free verse)*

» ***Blind judging*** *by the final judge*

» ***Final Judge****: A.E. Stallings*

» ***Entry Deadline:*** *March 31, 2016*

**GUIDELINES & ENTRY INFORMATION
AVAILABLE ONLINE AT:**

www.ablemusepress.com

AbleMUSE
A REVIEW OF POETRY, PROSE & ART

After more than a decade of online publishing excellence, Able Muse began a bold new chapter with its Print Edition

Check out our 12+ years of online archives for work by

RACHEL HADAS • X.J. KENNEDY • TIMOTHY STEELE • MARK JARMAN • A.E. STALLINGS • DICK DAVIS • A.M. JUSTER • TIMOTHY MURPHY • ANNIE FINCH • DEBORAH WARREN • CHELSEA RATHBURN • RHINA P. ESPAILLAT • TURNER CASSITY • RICHARD MOORE • STEPHEN EDGAR • DAVID MASON • THAISA FRANK • NINA SCHUYLER • N.S. THOMPSON • SOLITAIRE MILES • MISHA GORDIN • AND OTHERS

SUBSCRIPTION
Able Muse – Print Edition

Able Muse is published semiannually.
Subscription rates—for individuals: $24.00 per year; single and previous issues: $16.95 + $3 S&H.

International subscription rates: $33 per year; single and previous issues: $16.95 + $5 S&H. (USD throughout.)

Subscribe online with WePay/credit card at
www.ablemusepress.com

Or send a check payable to *Able Muse Review*

Attn: Alex Pepple – Editor, *Able Muse*, 467 Saratoga Avenue #602, San Jose, CA 95129 USA

CONTENTS

Alexander Pepple
 Editorial / v

ESSAYS

N.S. Thompson
 Unlocking the Shades in Duddingston Loch: Two Poems by a Contemporary Scottish Poet / 8

Moira Egan
 Vamp, Volta, Vows / 32

BOOK REVIEWS

Stephen Kampa
 Meeting David Foster Wallace for the First Time (Again) A Review of David Foster Wallace, *Both Flesh and Not: Essays* / 43

Robert B. Shaw
 A Review of Catherine Breese Davis, *On the Life and Work of an American Master* / 110

FEATURED POET

Amit Majmudar
 Interviewed by Daniel Brown / 81

POEMS

 No Future / 90
 Excerpt from an Intelligence Hearing / 91
 Chronic Pain / 92
 Protest Poem / 93
 The Strike-Anywhere Match / 94

Joachim du Bellay
 (*translated by Amit Majmudar*)
 Roman Holiday / 95

FEATURED ARTIST

Léon Leijdekkers
    A Photographic Exhibit / 51   Artist Statement / 52

ARTWORK
- Abbey Light / 53
- Church Rock, Study #2 / 54
- Commodious Sacrament / 55
- Connemara / 56
- Derelict Dream / 57
- Homage to Martin Henson / 58
- L'Île du Guesclin / 59
- Journey to No End / 60
- Les Braves / 61
- Lighthouse / 62
- The Cloister, One Late Afternoon / 63
- In the Crypt #3 / 64
- Oosterscheldekering, Study #3 / 65
- Pentre Ifan, Study #1 / 66
- L'Abbaye de Pontigny / 67
- Risin og Kellingin / 68
- Sanctuary / 69
- Sea Wall / 70
- Secluded Confidence / 71
- The Curve / 72

FICTION

Paul Soto
    Polaroid / 73

Lynda Sexson
    Why Were You Sighing? / 96

2015 Write Prize for Fiction · Winner

Andrea Witzke Slot
    After Reading the News Story of a Woman Who Attempted to Carry Her Dead Baby onto an Airplane / 37

2015 Write Prize for Poetry · Finalists

Jeanne Wagner
    On Watching a *Cascade* Commercial / 40

Elise Hempel
    The Jockey / 41

2015 Write Prize for Poetry · Winner

Elise Hempel
    Cathedral Peppersauce / 42

POETRY

Leslie Schultz
    VISAGE / *1*

Ryan Wilson
    XENIA / *2*

Max Gutmann
    OLD GROWTH / *4*

Freeman Rogers
    APOLOGY / *6*

Kim Bridgford
    THE FENCE / *7*

Peter Kline
    MIRRORFORM / *16*
    MIRRORFORM / *17*

Dan Campion
    NOIR / *18*

Brooke Clark
    ON FALSE DREAMS / *19*

X.J. Kennedy
    ON *ASPERITY STREET* / *20*

Wendy Videlock
    LIGHTLY SLEEPING ARE / *21*
    THE HOLE IN MY SHOE / *22*
    AT THE BASE OF QUANDARY PEAK / *24*

David Stephenson
    LINCOLN BARBER COLLEGE / *26*

Terese Coe
    MARKET INSTRUMENT / *28*

Autumn Newman
    SHOPPING WITH WHITNEY HOUSTON / *29*

Jennifer Reeser
    A WAIL FROM THE WILD POTATO CLAN ARBOR / *30*

James Matthew Wilson
    WOMAN AT WAWASEE / *31*

Athar C. Pavis
    ODE TO SILENCE / *100*

Catharine Savage Brosman
    THE PIANIST AND THE CICADA / *102*

Steven Winn
    THE PURPOSE OF THIS OBJECT IS NOT CERTAIN / *104*

Jay Udall
    TOOLS OF THE TRADE / *106*

Beth Houston
    ICE / *107*
    THE GHOST NUDGES ME TO THE CELLAR / *108*

TRANSLATION NOTES / *121*
CONTRIBUTOR NOTES / *127*
INDEX / *133*

New from

Slingshots and Love Plums
poems by **Wendy Videlock**
978-1-927409-52-7 | Paperback

". . . delicious variety of treats, from witty send-ups of contemporary mores to somber reflections on mortality, love, and friendship."
—David Caplan

". . . what begins as a taste for her work can quickly turn into a craving."
—David J. Rothman (from the foreword)

"… taking delight equally in huge abstraction and intimate real-worldliness."
—Maryann Corbett

". . . Playfully wise, sharp-tongued, and surprising as ever, *Slingshots and Love Plums* is yet another treasure to be read."
—Timothy Green

Bad Fame
poems by **Martin McGovern**
978-1-927409-50-3 | Paperback

"Martin McGovern's long-awaited, well-constructed first book gives itself away slowly, artfully. It is carefully considered, quietly passionate, and deeply humane.
—Edward Hirsch

"There is an unforsaken paradise in these pages, and a lot of ungodly anxiety."
—David Lazar (from the foreword)

". . . the sentences, like the centuries, are treated pitilessly, as you can hear, yet there is what the poet calls "the shimmer of a teen movie" throughout. Resilient art, and no loitering."
—Richard Howard

Details at

ABLE MUSE PRESS

Asperity Street
Poems by Gail White
978-1-927409-54-1 | Paperback

"With her sublime linguistic choreography, these poems dance to complex metrical tunes. We feel and hear them pulse with equal parts sympathy and vitriol."
— Molly Peacock
   (Judge, 2014 Able Muse Book Award)

". . . another collection by one of America's wittiest, most technically adept, funniest and most serious commentators on what it feels like to be human."
— Rhina P. Espaillat (from the foreword)

". . . a serious poet I'd not encountered before: there was a deepening of vision . . . a cutting edge that slices to the bone. Don't miss reading this book."
— Lewis Turco

Times Square and Other Stories
by William Baer
978-1-927409-43-5 | Paperback

". . . a serious collection of short stories! . . . broadminded, large-hearted, sharply observed, and dryly, obliquely funny."
—Pinckney Benedict

". . . the effort that undoubtedly went into their composition could easily be overlooked due to the skill with which they are rendered, and the degree to which they are enjoyed."
—A.G. Harmon

"These fictions resuscitate Poe's unities of effects, breathing life back into the simulacrum of life. I loved this book; it can't help but blurb itself!"
—Michael Martone

www.AbleMusePress.com

Taking Shape
Carmina Figurata
by Jan D. Hodge

*NEW~ from Able Muse Press

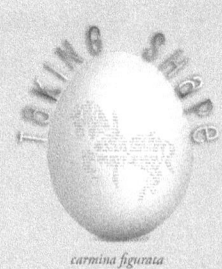

80 pages
ISBN 978-1-927409-56-5 (paperback)
ISBN 978-1-927409-58-9 (hardcover)

PRAISE FOR *TAKING SHAPE*

The first full-length collection from Jan D. Hodge

★★★★★

"In Jan D. Hodge's Taking Shape *the subjects have burst from their cages and confront us immediately with what they are. Then the words they are made of can reveal their inner beings.*"
— Fred Chappell

"*Through a wide-ranging array of subjects and tones, Hodge's mastery of language within such challenging constraints is truly impressive. Syntax and rhythm, metaphor and symbol (see for instance "The One That Got Away" or "The Lesson of the Snow"), conversational snippets and quatrains, are surprisingly nuanced.*"
— Robert J. Conley

"*Jan D. Hodge is the master par excellence of carmina figurata . . . Hodge knows of grace, his poems are full of grace, and* Taking Shape, *like grace itself, is a gift of utter beauty.*"
— Vince Gotera

ORDER NOW FROM ABLE MUSE PRESS AT: WWW.ABLEMUSEPRESS.COM
OR, ORDER FROM AMAZON.COM, BN.COM & OTHER ONLINE OR OFFLINE BOOKSTORES

www.AbleMusePress.com

Congratulations to the 2015 *Able* MUSE CONTEST WINNERS

2015 ABLE MUSE WRITE PRIZE

FICTION
Final Judge: **Eugenia Kim**

WINNER
Andrea Witzke Slot
"After Reading the News Story of a Woman Who Attempted to Carry Her Dead Baby onto an Airplane"

HONORABLE MENTION
James Cooper
Albert Liau

POETRY
Final Judge: **H.L. Hix**

WINNER
Elise Hempel
"Cathedral Peppersauce"

FINALISTS
Elise Hempel: "Jockey"

Jeanne Wagner: "On Watching a Cascade Commercial"

SHORTLIST
- Jim Bartruff • Midge Goldberg
- Trish Lindsey Jaggers • Miriam O'Neal • Gabriel Spera • Marty Steyer • M.K. Sukach

2015 ABLE MUSE BOOK AWARD

POETRY MANUSCRIPT
Final Judge: **Peter Campion**

WINNER
Emily Leithauser
The Borrowed World

FINALISTS
- Katie Hartsock: *Bed of Impatiens*
- Elise Hempel: *Second Rain*
- Alfred Nicol: *Animal Psalms*

SHORTLIST
- Jeanne Emmons: *The Forming House*
- Rob Griffith: *The Devil in the Milk*
- Patricia Hooper: *Separate Flights*
- Jean L. Kreiling: *Arts & Letters & Love*
- Brad Aaron Modlin: *Everyone at This Party Has Two Names*
- Rob Wright: *Holding on to the Hard Earth*

BOOKS FROM SOME OF THE FINALIST AUTHORS ALSO COMING SOON FROM ABLE MUSE PRESS!

Cause for Concern
Poems
by Carrie Shipers

*NEW~ *from* Able Muse Press

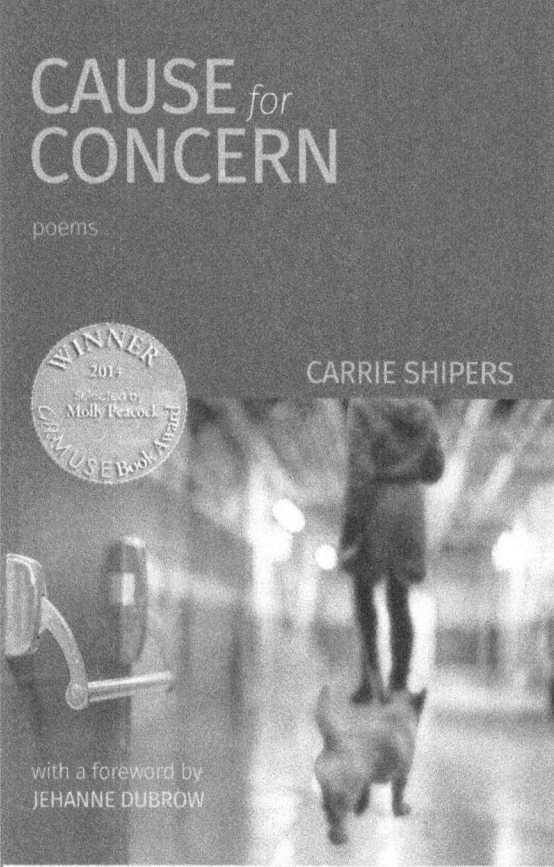

WINNER
2014 Able Muse Book Award

PRAISE FOR *CAUSE FOR CONCERN*
(with an foreword by Jehanne Dubrow)

Full-length collection from Carrie Shipers

★★★★★

"Shipers reminds us that our lives must first be prodded and cauterized, if the injured parts are ever to heal."
— Jehanne Dubrow

"Her poet's craft, palpable in every arresting line, makes the subtlest turns of vulnerability with enviable poise."
— Molly Peacock
(Judge, 2014 Able Muse Book Award)

". . . such exquisite, irresistible and terrifying honesty."
— Kwame Dawes

ISBN 978-1-927409-59-6 / 106 pages
ORDER NOW FROM ABLE MUSE PRESS AT: WWW.ABLEMUSEPRESS.COM
OR, ORDER FROM AMAZON.COM, BN.COM & OTHER ONLINE OR OFFLINE BOOKSTORES

www.AbleMusePress.com

Leslie Schultz

Visage

for W.S., in response

In me you see the beauty of a flower
that, once admired, withers in the vase;
whose dewy blush is dimmed each passing hour,
whose rouge sets florid on a wrinkled face.

In me you see an artful setting sun
whose colors cling to venoms in the air;
a moment trembling, before the light is done,
that kisses dust and makes the dust seem fair.

My face must seem the rising of a moon,
a profile gaunt and silver set in black,
a cameo of stained and carved bone,
a mask whose features have begun to crack.

Look closely at the clench of futile rage:
I'm now a woman of a certain age.

Ryan Wilson

Xenia

One day a silent man arrives
At your door in an outdated suit,
Threadbare and black, like a lost mourner
Or a Bible salesman who's been robbed.
Penniless, he needs a place to stay.
And you, magnanimous you, soon find
This stranger reading in your chair,
Eating your cereal, drinking your tea,
Or standing in your clothes at the window
Awash in afternoon's alien light.

You tire of his constant company.
Your floorboards creak with his shuffling footfalls,
Haunting dark rooms deep in the night.
You lie awake in blackness, listening,
Cursing the charity or pride
That opened up the door for him
And wonder how to explain yourself.
He smells like durian and smoke
But it's mostly his presence, irksome, fogging
The mind up like breath on a mirror . . .

You practice cruelty in a mirror,
Then practice sympathetic faces.
You ghoul. Your cunning can't deceive you.
You are afraid to call your friends
For help, knowing what they would say.
It's just you two. You throw a fit when
He sneaks water into the whisky bottle,
Then make amends. You have no choice
Except to learn humility,
To love this stranger as yourself,

Who won't love you, or ever leave.

Max Gutmann

Old Growth

So rooted
seem couples to a child! Firm-trunked and tall.
Some scrawny: sparsely leaved or badly fruited,
but fixed and solid, works of nature all.
It challenges imagination
that choice was part of the creation.

That they,
these halves, weren't mingled always, childhood fails
to comprehend. The stories of the way
one's parents met are magic, fairy tales.
To know the seed becomes the tree
does not dispel the mystery.

Divorce,
unless it strikes our parents, flashes where
it cannot burst our faith. A sudden force
that leaves the broken trunks deformed but there,
disaster-stricken, strangely ill,
but giving partial shelter still.

We feel
this all collapse as childhood's shed. The trees
we thought so firm and fixed were never real.
To navigate by them can only tease.
Whatever fantasies persist,
unmoving couples don't exist.

To find
one's half and gather height and leaves are less
like acts of nature than like hiking blind.
Soil shifts and landmarks vanish. We must guess,
our one-time orchard morphing to
a wood no map can guide us through.

Freeman Rogers

Apology

Mr. Brown, we've let
your old field go.
Your great-great-greats first cleared their debt
here, planting the rows

of corn, the fescue,
and the apple trees
on land you worked until a stroke forced you
to sell at eighty-three.

Now, we cultivate a subtle bristle
to hold eroding
clay: mowing once a year keeps thistle
blooms exploding,
our only harvest an entire
field of purple fire.

Kim Bridgford

The Fence

One day, it seems they all looked old.
One day, it seems it didn't matter.
One day, it seems what once was gold
Was really not. The something better

You always thought was coming next
Was like the rumored farthest hill.
Why was it just the same again?
Why was the optimism shrill?

Why did you then look up and see
How people came and people went,
And no one cared? But meanwhile money
Bought the system, and what it meant.

You lived your life in innocence,
And had a pretty child. You wept.
They depend on folks like you. The fence?
It grew around you while you slept.

ESSAY

N.S. Thompson

Unlocking the Shades in Duddingston Loch: Two Poems by a Contemporary Scottish Poet

The Reverend Robert Walker Skating on Duddingston Loch
  By David Kinloch

The water tensed at his instruction
and trout gazed up at his incisive feet.
We felt that God must be in clarity like this
and listened to the dull glens echo
the striations of his silver blades.

Far out on Duddingston Loch
our true apostle sped
with twice the speed of Christ
who walked on waves.

We saw him harrow ice
with the grace of the elect
and scar the transubstantiation
of wintered elements.

With a sense of real presence
he crossed our loch
what need of vestments
with such elegant legs?

(1985)

Young Blade
    By David Kinloch

Moonlight becomes blades, blades moonlight as they lilt and pivot out of shadow
into yellow pools: I make a point and stop:

steam breath into air that cracks like ice,
close eyes upon a world that gleams
and scrapes and rasps; "Look out!"

Brown, behatted, a figure grasps
my arm and birls me about; I make a run:
circling to the centre of the loch—

cross stroke, chassé, cross over slip—turn
and look back across the white and shining
field: the huddle of "ingénues"

practising their 8's, the cries of "off!"
and "change!," the silver scales
of safety ropes slithering from baskets;

silence set off by distant swish.

And so I see the scene again: late
afternoon; the little minister, still svelte
but on the verge of portliness, breasting
the ice with frank and open stroke;

his friends, the painters, smiling, betting:
which one could lay down just that shade
of lilac shadow cast by suburban
Mercury, silhouetted *contre jour?*

Then, the sudden hush as water is tensed
at his instruction, trout gazed up at his incisive feet.
I felt that God must be in clarity like this
and listened to the valley echo

the striations of his silver blades.
Far out on Duddingston Loch
our true apostle sped with twice the speed
of Christ who walked on waves.

I saw him harrow ice with grace of the elect
and scar the transubstantiation
of wintered elements. At once I heard
a tapping from the hills

as if a tiny hammer big with work
sought to split this world: the shelf
of ice with all its merry skaters
cracked from side to side then tipped

like a sinking ship; loch made
meadow loch as little cows,
aristocratic blades, the Reverend
and his painters clung to trees

above a sundered castle, floated off
to villages, new towns, enlightened
schemes and sunken moonlit pastures.
With a sense of real presence

he crossed my vision: and I wondered
if it mattered which man would win
the bet: Raeburn or Danloux?

Both helped him to untie
the fine pink inkles strapping blade
to boot and walked away with him

arm in arm towards the village.

(2011)

★★★

I

The late Donald Justice identified "Platonic shades" as a source of inspiration in his work, where a prior text led directly or indirectly to a poem of his own. This was not akin to a translation in any sense, although Justice did use translations (both his own and those of others) in his work. It was more an overarching presence that inspired the creation of a new poem. Examining this process is not so much the traditional literary task of source hunting as identifying the use and transformation of the text in the creation of the new work. Readers of the urtext of Eliot's *The Waste Land* (*A facsimile and transcript of the original drafts* edited by Valerie Eliot) will have an understanding of what this means, except that in the case of Eliot's poem the editing and suggestions made by both Pound and Vivien Eliot provoked the poet to develop the poem, rather than the poet's own stimulus.

In reading a recent collection by the contemporary Scottish poet David Kinloch *Finger of a Frenchman* (Carcanet, 2011), I was struck by a poem that had echoes of one by the same poet I remembered reading many years previously in an earlier anthology[1]. The two poems are printed above and this essay will discuss the "Platonic shade" of the first on the second and also act as a salutary reminder that poetry may appear to be Wordsworth's "spontaneous overflow of powerful feelings," but is more often the result of revision, patient craft and sometimes even the revisitation of an earlier work.

Firstly, a little background. The two poems refer to two paintings made more than sixty years apart, but closely connected in subject matter. *The Reverend Robert Walker Skating on Duddingston Loch* (c. 1795), also known as *The Skating Minister,* is a small painting once attributed to Sir Henry Raeburn that hangs in Scotland's National Gallery in Edinburgh. The subject was a member of the Edinburgh Skating Club, the oldest figure skating club in the world. In recent years the attribution of this iconic painting of the Scottish Enlightenment has been questioned (on good grounds) with a preferred attribution now of the émigré French painter Henri-Pierre Danloux. More than fifty years later a pupil of Raeburn, Charles Lees, also painted two scenes of the Edinburgh Skating Club on the Loch, and Kinloch refers to the second of the two, *Skaters: Duddingston Loch by Moonlight* (1857) a work which hangs in the Fleming Collection, London.

The first poem is a witty ekphrastic study that focuses on the charming figure of the minister as he glides effortlessly on one foot in traveling position over the ice, his body curved almost in a bow as he proceeds from left to right across the picture. In the figurative language of the poem the minister is seen as a type of Christ walking on the waters, "our

---

[1] *Other Tongues: Young Scottish Poets in English, Scots and Gaelic,* edited by Robert Crawford (St Andrews: Verse, 1990), p. 21. It was first published in *Lines Review,* 102, September 1987, p. 29 and subsequently published in the poet's first collection, *Paris-Forfar* (Edinburgh: Polygon, 1994), p.1.

true apostle of speed," and also in comic exaggeration as the Harrower of Hell: "We saw him harrow ice/ with the grace of the elect." The conceits here build on the figure's clerical status and the view reflects the admiration of his fellow skaters watching the performance. The sense of play culminates in the pun of the minister as he "crossed" the loch, almost in benediction. Finally, the observation that he has no need of clerical "vestments" with "such elegant legs" undercuts the preceding conceits and brings us back to the real physical Robert Walker. It is a delightful poem, skillfully handled.

In "Young Blade" the first five stanzas place the speaker of this poem clearly in the middle of the crowded group scene of Lees's *Skaters: Duddingston Loch by Moonlight*. Color and action are made more vivid by the use of technical terms for the various figures the skaters perform. Then at line 17, we have what could be called a *volta,* a "turn" in perspective as expected in the traditional sonnet between the octave and the sestet. Philip Larkin does something similar in the "The Whitsun Weddings" when he looks more closely at the wedding groups getting onto the train:

> Struck, I leant
> More promptly out next time, more curiously,
> *And saw it all again in different terms:*
>   (my emphasis)

In "Young Blade," the poem's persona has described himself as one of the group of skaters in the moonlight, but then recalls an earlier scene, that of the "The Skating Minister" and also, as we will shortly see, Kinloch's earlier poem:

> And so I see the scene again: late
> afternoon; the little minister, still svelte
> but on the verge of portliness, breasting
> the ice with a frank and open stroke. . . .

The poet adds to this scene by having the persona imagine the minister's artist friends (Raeburn and Danloux) having a wager on who can paint "the suburban/ Mercury" in the right shade of color. But then interestingly the persona recalls the actual lines of the earlier poem, the first person plural of the original becoming singular:

> Then, the sudden hush as water tensed
> at his instruction, trout gazed up at his incisive feet.
> I felt that God must be in clarity like this
> and listened to the valley echo
>
> the striations of his silver blades.
>   ("Young Blade," ll. 25-29)

> cf.
> The water tensed at his instruction
> and trout gazed up at his incisive feet.
> We felt that God must be in clarity like this
> and listened to the dull glens echo
> the striations of his silver blades.
>   ("The Reverend Robert Walker," ll. 1-5)

And so it continues: lines 6-13 are repeated almost exactly except for the change of person, the "glens" becoming a "valley," and the lineation:

> Far out on Duddingston Loch
> our true apostle sped with twice the speed
> of Christ who walked on waves.
>
> I saw him harrow ice with grace of the elect
> and scar transubstantiation
> of wintered elements.
>   ("Young Blade," ll. 30-35)

> cf.
> Far out on Duddingston Loch
> our true apostle sped
> with twice the speed of Christ
> who walked the waves.
>
> We saw him harrow ice
> with grace of the elect
> and scar transubstantiation
> of wintered elements.
>   ("Reverend Robert Walker," ll. 6-13)

By only a few changes, we can see the light touch of the first poem transformed into a more serious mode brought about by the dramatic addition of "the sudden hush [as water tensed]." A simple addition, but one that radically changes the effect of lines formerly used in a more lighthearted manner. And the rest of the poem bears this out. The speaker hears "a tapping from the hills" which attempts to split the skaters' world like the very ice they are skating on. The following lines remind me of a Chagall painting where many of the people and animals end up in trees: a dream apocalypse, a world seen after the Flood? Perhaps these figures fly into the air like the characters at the end of *Alice in Wonderland*, floating off "to villages, new towns." But this strange splitting of the vision brings the image of the Reverend Robert Walker clearly back to the speaker's mind as he wonders which among the watching painters will win the wager of being able to paint "just that shade/ of lilac shadow cast by the suburban/Mercury" and asks "Raeburn or Danloux?" But the question is rhetorical, unanswered. In a charming vision of unity the persona sees both the Scottish and the French painter helping the minister off with his blades—tied by their delicate "inkles"—and walking with him arm in arm towards the village.

And what to make of the interpolation, as it were, of the scene "tipped// like a sinking ship" (ll. 30-47)? Is it comic or serious? There are two possibilities of reading the passage and they both connect. Firstly one can see the apocalyptic view as the result of the minister's harrowing of "the wintered elements," upturning the tranquil scene. At the same time, the man's "real presence" seems to calm the disruption, as if again he were a Christ walking on the waters and bringing a calm to the vision (cf. *Mark* 6, and later Gospels). The world turned upside down here could also reflect aspects of the Industrial Revolution, with its "new towns" and "enlightened schemes" such as the industrialist Robert Owen pioneered in New Lanark and envisaged elsewhere.

Whatever the case, this dream vision serves to contrast with the peacefulness of the preceding scene and emphasizes the impact of the minister as his passing over the ice again brings a sense of closure and of calm.

II

A fascinating aspect of these two poems, particularly the image of the minister that is repeated in the second (ll. 29-39), is the richness of the religious metaphors in the creation of the main conceit. The Reverend is an "apostle" with "twice the speed of Christ" who harrows the ice "with the grace of the elect" as he scars "the transubstantiation of wintered elements." All told they create the figure of effortless command over the winter landscape; or at the very least, he is in harmony with it. If he instructs the ice, it is more his audience who is being given a lesson in grace, playing on the meaning of physical elegance against divine favor. This contrast is pointed to in the opposition of (clerical) vestments against "elegant legs." The point of all this elevated language is indeed to elevate the minister in our eyes as an admirable figure whose grace has the ability to teach, recalling Hemingway's famous definition of courage as "grace under pressure," especially in physical circumstances.

Perhaps this ministry has another Platonic shade in Wordsworth's famous skating episode of *The Prelude* (I, 452-489, 1805-6 version) where the poet details all the teaching that Nature gave him, as he says several lines later:

> Ye Presences of Nature in the sky
> Or on the earth! Ye Visions of the hills!
> And Souls of lonely places! can I think
> A vulgar hope was yours when ye employed
> Such ministry. . . .
>
> (I, ll. 490-94)

One feels that if the minister in these poems has something to teach it is because he has absorbed Wordsworth's feelings, or rather Kinloch has endowed him with such a capability, recalling the preface to the *Lyrical Ballads* (1800) where Wordsworth defends the everyday subject matter of his poems "from common life" but also says that his intention was

> to throw over them a certain colouring of the imagination, whereby ordinary things should be presented to the mind in an unusual aspect . . . to make these incidents and situations interesting by tracing in them . . . the primary laws of our nature. . . .

Later he says of the poems that "the feeling therein developed gives importance to the action and situation, and not the action and situation to the feeling."

The richness of coloring that the contemporary poet has given to the simple depiction of a late eighteenth-century skater (and Lees's later skaters) is a perfect example of Wordsworth's meaning. He has created a verbal picture that goes way beyond what Raeburn or Danloux or Lees depicted and so added a "feeling therein" that adumbrates and adds meaning to the original image(s). In sum, he creates depth and resonance in the image by imbuing it with a layering of Platonic shades from his earlier work and with perhaps more than a touch of Romantic theory.

Peter Kline

Mirrorform

    Written into absence
    certain words explode,
    strewing their starry payload
    in morphemed radiance

    each time they join. What chance
    have we to spark like that
    before our verse is set,
    written into absence?

Peter Kline

Mirrorform

> Desires ungratified
> Persist from one life to the next.
> —James Merrill, *The Kimono*

Desires ungratified
break down into the flesh,
tangling in the mesh
of plaited nucleotides.

Some spike the lymph, or blood.
Others, more benign,
put kinks in the family line
who can't be gratified.

Dan Campion

Noir

At midnight, flashing blue slides up the shade,
raised voices complicate the street. The cops
are questioning some kid. A motorcade
of cruisers hugs the curb. The drama stops
on "disappointed," audible despite
a barking dog, which someone says inside
a tight white arc of otherworldly light
that focuses the show on just one slide.
At last somebody lights a cigarette,
a bunch of car doors slam, quiet's restored,
the audience permitted to forget,
indifferent to what blotter may record.
No Icarus, no ocean, not a splash,
just ordinary scoring by the lash.

Brooke Clark

On False Dreams

    Ross claims to envy poets their life of carefree penury,
        but lives amid the best things money can buy,
  which he dismisses with a wave blasé as any duke's—
        no doubt he thinks God's words were, "Fiat luxe"—
  and says that no one understands the burden wealth can be.
        To envy the poor is a rich man's luxury.

X.J. Kennedy

On *Asperity Street*

For Gail White

Having just read *Asperity*
   Street, each line, every word,
I'm both kinds of martini,
   Not only shaken but stirred.

How gracefully it assuages
   Pain of babe, adolescent, wife—
Whoever opens its pages
   Touches an entire life.

Most poetry now that the best invent
   Winds will scatter in a day,
But you give us a towering testament
   That refuses to go away.

Wendy Videlock

Lightly Sleeping Are

    Lightly sleeping are
            the queens of bees,
              the tic-tock gods,
         the lunar bloom,
       the ape of hearts,
      their bodies
        forming

      cosmic little
      question marks.

Wendy Videlock

The Hole in My Shoe

There appears to be a hole in my shoe

says the old to the new
and what will you do
when under the influence

of the moon
and what have you gleaned

said the light to the gloom—

an inquiry
or a sordid boon, a victory scree

or the keening room,
and what what will you say

when they come for your dust

with a mop and a rag
and an old broom

and what of the moon

and what will you leave
when you've plunged to your depths

or leapt to your feet

said the hole in my shoe

said the hole in my shoe

on the night of the moon

to the old and the new.

Wendy Videlock

At the Base of Quandary Peak
for Belle Turnbull

Here see
wasps
and beetles
even skeeters
miners
weepers even
keelers smoke

and mirror
song
and teacher
knowledge-
leaper
word

and cedar
scrub
and cleaner
olly olly
oxen

freers,

cough
and groan

caw
of crow
thunder

bolt—

loads
of gold—

spirit innit?—

flesh and bone.

David Stephenson

Lincoln Barber College

The theory was the students had to cut
A fixed number of heads before they got
Their barber's license. So there was a stir
When Dad and Bill and Bob and I came through
The creaking door they'd rigged up with a bell.

The novices in the dollar seats up front
Would stand up smiling and shake out their smocks,
But Dad would steer us into the back room,
Over the hair-strewn linoleum,
To the two-dollar senior student chairs.

The choices were the Butch, a straight buzz cut,
Or the Princeton, where they left you with
A stylish forelock. Bob and I got butched
Without thought, but Bill was a Princeton man
And the possessor of a pocket comb.

The talk was mostly weather, high school sports,
Cars, farm prices, jokes, and TV shows.
They had hot rod and hunting magazines.
They always asked Dad how things were at Deere
And whether or not it was a contract year.

But there wasn't much talk driving home,
Piled in the back seat of the Pontiac,
Hee Haw music on the radio,
The windows rolled down, scooping in the air,
The wind figuratively in our hair—

Past the high school and the Baptist church,
The cemetery and the Planter Works
Looming behind fences and guard shacks,
Over the viaduct and railroad tracks,
Up the big hill and no looking back.

Terese Coe

Market Instrument

He has a slight existence,
expectant but mundane,
consciousness, futility,
the hoards without the gain

a cage of obligations,
then lagging revenue
till afternoon brings figures
that he cannot construe.

And night falls on the margin
when all the whiskey's poured,
and slices like a surgeon,
and when you're dead you're cured.

Autumn Newman

Shopping with Whitney Houston

Thrift store shopping is better than crack. I warm
up with a casual inspection of
the "Home Goods," picking up the tiny worn
Chinese vase somebody used to love.
When I hit "Ladies Shirts," endorphins peak.
Cacophony of sliding hangers, metal
hooks on metal bars, and then the meek
tick of plastic against plastic. I settle
into my high. Until I hear, lapping at
the brackish, foamy, glass-flecked shores of my head,
a song. My hum is automatic and flat:
with somebody who loves me and then, like lead
in a pillowcase upside my head, I see
the headlines, never the ones I thought I'd see.

Then other headlines, smaller ones, about me.
I see his wide blue eyes and hear his voice,
atonal, almost whispered, *you're gonna fuck me,
again.* His fist waits, as if I have a choice,
then softens to a strangle around my neck.
Thirteen years I tried to drink away
those vapid hands, but all I got was sick.
So I understood her willowy display
on *People* magazine, but most people ask
such stupid questions about drugs and fame
and love. They mistook the woman for the mask,
Incapable of reading past her name.
A screeching hanger snaps the moment back,
to the basement smell, the vase with its tiny crack.

Jennifer Reeser

A Wail from the Wild Potato Clan Arbor

Which one will ever know of this and value you?
"No one, no one, not ever," vows the mockingbird.
"No one, no one, forever. Every pretty word
Will serve to praise another in your place," they coo.
"Unnoted till the end of time," intones the shrew.
The pewter wings of pigeons wave—"Unheard, unheard!"
A feather is dispersed each beat as air is stirred.
"Not only now but evermore. Adieu! Adieu!"
"Because you chose the rose-free, thorn-inviting road,"
The stones admonish me, "your role will be forgotten . . ."
"Forgotten, yes!" picks up and croaks the moldy toad.
The mushrooms of the forest, too—spore-marked and rotten—
Spit disapproval in my face, and then explode
Within my gathered skirt, to scorch its orchid cotton.

James Matthew Wilson

Woman at Wawasee

I

The white swans on the water, gliding, three
Of them, and you posed on the dock, and me,
Looking out from the seaweed-covered sand
At you as white as marble and meant to be.

II

She didn't think that we would last so long.
I drank and stayed out late and got along
With any bored slug slouched against the bar.
She'd underestimated, but wasn't wrong.

III

A thousand images of you in sun-
Or candle-light would stir near anyone
To change his life. But easier for desire
To turn a marble girl a living one.

ESSAY

Moira Egan
Vamp, Volta, Vows

It's called a "crown" of sonnets because the final line of the sequence repeats the very first line of the sequence, bringing the poems full circle.

Don't get me wrong: I wasn't entirely in the habit of spending afternoons in Fells Point bars. There I sat with a pint of Guinness in the Cat's Eye, that venerable old waterfront establishment in Baltimore, enjoying the sun sparkling on the dirty harbor water, the spring breeze wafting in, carrying with it pink blossoms and stinky, bluish cigar smoke.

Exhausted from teaching, a little hungover, I looked in the bar mirror and saw a face that could hardly be mistaken, as had often been the case, for being ten years younger than it actually was.

Some lines floated down to me:

> The face I'm seeing in the bar's back mirror
> looks tired and just my age, I hate to say,
> as if I need a sign that's any clearer . . .

I scribbled them quickly on a cocktail napkin with my trusty purple Pilot Precise V-5, perfect on the absorbent yet slightly resistant paper.

Iambic pentameter comes naturally because it embodies the rhythm of the human heartbeat: lub-DUB.

My attention flitted back and forth between the seed of the sonnet I was writing and the slightly seedy glamour of the professional barflies who populated the length of the polished oak bar. When the right song came on, they'd hit the dance floor. The bearded big-bellied guy, Central Casting for Jack Sparrow in his sixties. The still-attractive, skinny blond, makeup artfully if heavily applied, wiggling Seventies-style in tight red, boot-cut jeans. I'd met these people, I was sure, when I was a teenager and my father used to bring me along with him.

When I was sixteen, I passed for twenty-one.

Numbers. I did the math that day. I had been dating (don't fall off your barstool) for thirty years. Three full decades of falling in and out of love, of leaving and being left, of dancing, kissing, missing. How many stories? How many missteps, how many agonized skips in the lub-DUB rhythm of my heart?

Alexander Pope was making fun of silly critics when he said that "most by numbers judge a poet's song;/ And smooth or rough, with them is right or wrong." But I'm a poet, and I write sonnets (yes, I know, that and $3.75 will get me a *caffe latte* at Starbuck's): didn't I just have the smooth and the rough, the right and the wrong to write about. Thirty years' worth. That afternoon, the Bar Napkin Sonnets were conceived.

For months, I had fun transforming the "Sex and the City"-like incidents of a single girl into sonnets. Exploits real and imagined, "facts" sometimes slightly embroidered to fit the requirements of the form, the rhyme and the meter. A hot-wings-at-the-bar scene featured a completely invented Englishman, created because, once the fellow's pick-up line was written in iambs, he sounded British. "He said, 'Though you look comfortable alone,/ I'll sit here, if you've no objection, Love.'" A bit of flash fiction, then, containing, in that way that fiction does, some truths, or Truth, including a meditation on border crossings of various sorts.

Many borders crossed. Transgressed. The sonnet has its origins in the thirteenth-century courts of Sicily and, due to its wonderful, compact shape and its useful malleability, bending but not breaking with the flow of history and cultures, it's still with us after all these years. Most contemporary poets don't write sonnets. Poets and non-poets alike look at me quizzically when I confess that I write these seemingly archaic, rhymed and metered fourteen-liners.

I like the challenge. I like restraints.

It was fun to write these sonnets with a stance that would be called *macho* if I'd happened to have been born a man. It was fun to prance in poems in stilettos that I hadn't worn in years, to get into trouble at a whiskey bar, to seduce the fictional bartender who realizes that The Date, once again, is late. It was fun to throw in as many literary allusions as I could, giggling and wondering if dead poets spin in their graves when their imagery is so willfully and blissfully misappropriated. Or appropriated in the service of some other force of nature: "sweet Bacchus's pards" conjured up in a shot of tequila. Several shots.

Dante had his Beatrice, Petrarch his lovely Laura; these gentlemen perfected the art of writing sonnets in the voice of the desperately desiring man speaking to the unattainable woman, the Lady on her Pedestal. Shakespeare shook up that soon-staled model, writing naughty sonnets to the beautiful boy and the mysterious dark lady. Many women, too, sat in their chambers and wrote sonnets, but when it was a woman expressing desire, this was the Lust that, for centuries, could not speak its Truth. Masks. Stances. Disguises.

The bad-girl speaker of the Bar Napkin Sonnets is tough. I usually talk about her in the third person, because she never was fully (and certainly now isn't) me. (Funny, isn't it: we don't immediately assume that the protagonist of a novel is a direct embodiment of its author, do we? But the "I" in a poem is all too often read as The Poet.) This speaker is tough, she's fiercely independent, and she's out for adventure in ways that might just elicit some scurrilous language. "Tonight *I thought as well him as another/* I'll Molly Bloom my way into his lair." If she can't be with the one she loves, she will love the one she's with.

Love? As many poets have written, sometimes the requirements of writing in form will take your imagination to a place it wouldn't have reached on its own. Sometimes it leads to questions you otherwise might not have asked. And sometimes a line break can kick you in the butt. "I want to fall in love, but not forever./ Is that the truth, or am I still confused/ where love's concerned? Or am I simply used/ to Solitary broken by Whoever/ looks interested or interesting? . . ."

Toward the end of a sonnet, there is traditionally the *volta:* a turn, a swerve, a new direction in thought.

As I was writing the final poems of my sequence, casting a cold eye on [very] raw material, crystallizing thoughts and desires, shaping them into something ordered and formal, I experienced a real-life *volta*. I loved the character who was embodied in these sonnets, her balls-to-the-wall pluck and resilience through the years of venturing from one "bachelor-silk cocoon" to another, wobbling home, traces of last night's makeup on her face. I loved her, I loved her wildness and her strength, but I was beginning to see ever more clearly the widening gulf between that bad-girl stance, that calloused heart, and what I actually wanted for myself.

And this I know, too: most people understand that the urge to find a partner, to make a Love Match, is perfectly acceptable, even—normal. Otherwise, why would we still be reading Jane Austen? But it's also true that a little Daddy's Girl who is left behind by that Daddy in a difficult divorce often spends her life attempting to heal that primal wound, trying to inveigle the stray-cat rockabilly guy she meets at CBGB into falling in love with her. This phenomenon has been amply documented by trained professionals.

If that's the diagnosis, then what is the cure? "Poet, heal thyself." Having come to this scary *volta,* my very own, late-blooming epiphany, *I want a genuine partner,* I set about cleaning up my act. Sometimes I stayed in on Friday nights. I thought twice about a potential date. Do we actually have things in common? Could I see myself with him five years down the road? Hmm, maybe not. Are we having a stupid conversation at dinner? "Can we see each other again?" Hmm, maybe not. I'm not saying I suddenly went all angelic or anything, but I tried to be careful with myself, with my heart.

Unlike their questing auntie, my lovely nieces took early to the idea that a suitable life partner might just be a nice thing. The first of my nieces to marry had a beautiful wedding on an island: happy guests, good food, great music, and the traditional tossing of the bridal bouquet. Skittering on my new Fluevogs, I was pushed out onto the dance floor with the other "single girls," all of whom were at least twenty years my junior. That bunch of flowers came hurtling toward me like an inevitable missile. My left hand shot up; I did Cal Ripken proud.

Click. It felt like an omen. Less than a month later, I met a very nice man. An Italian, a doctor by day who just happened, by night, to translate American poetry into Italian. Sweet, gentle, intelligent. Soon, he'd be going back to Rome. We spent every evening together.

A sonnet crown comes full circle, the final line of the sequence repeating the very first line.

We met for our last Happy Hour at the Cat's Eye. With a mischievous smile, he handed me a sheet of luscious, heavy card stock with something carefully lettered on it. It was one of my own poems, translated into Italian.

I almost wish I could say that that poem was a sonnet. It wasn't. But isn't that what a *volta* should do: bring about a change, carry one off to an entirely different place?

★ ★ ★

8

(Though poets lie in service of the truth
and fiction's simply truth tricked out in lies,
what do I tell my students, whose sweet youth
does not allow for gritty subtleties?
That I commit the crimes of one still young
and too immortal to obey what's best
for organs such as liver, heart, and tongue?
I keep my wild-hair story-box suppressed
—I love my kids—and though I feel unjust
I hope they'll understand me when they're old
enough to see that love's a blinding trust
that lives, or doesn't, once the lie's been told.
Therefore I lie to them, so I can be
a part of them, and yet hold on to me.)

11

Things happen when you drink too much mescal.
One night, with not enough food in my belly,
he kept on buying. I'm a girl who'll fall
damn near in love with gratitude and, well, he
was hot and generous and so the least
that I could do was let him kiss me, hard
and soft and *any way you want it*, beast
and beauty, lime and salt—sweet Bacchus' pards—
and when his friend showed up I felt so warm
and generous I let him kiss me too.
His buddy asked me if it was the worm
inside that makes me do the things I do.
I wasn't sure which worm he meant, the one
I ate? The one that eats at me alone?

24

It's wicked to admit I love these bruises,
the set of fingerprints along my hip
that an FBI Agent could dust and use
to track him down. I love the boy-stung lips
from hours kissing, lips soft, but his whiskers
grown rougher with the hours into night,
and rougher still, we move together, quicker,
as if our muscles' work brought on the light.
Mornings like this, I'm torn between two notions:
are love's inscriptions like a form of art,
or injuries incurred from constant motion—
tennis elbow, carpal tunnel, arrhythmic heart?
And *you should see my scars*. I sit alone,
a glass of wine, a napkin, and my pen.

ABLE MUSE WRITE PRIZE FOR FICTION, 2015 • WINNER

Andrea Witzke Slot

After Reading the News Story of a Woman Who Attempted to Carry Her Dead Baby onto an Airplane

Not long a mother, young and unsure of just what that meant, I threaded the aisle of the 747, ready to return to London, to my son, to my daughter, small and eager, asking on the phone, How much longer, Mommy? and How long is that?

Settling into my seat, I exchanged hellos with the man beside me and glanced down at the headlines of the newspaper on his knee: *Woman Arrested after Attempting to Carry Dead Baby onto Plane at JFK.*

I pulled my seat belt around me and felt my stomach drop as if we were already moving into flight.

Would you mind? I asked, daring to look down at the paper again.

No problem, he said, handing the paper to me.

Children in the plane cried as parents readied themselves for the journey ahead, bottles and toys and messes in laps, as others continued to file past, finding seats.

I smoothed the paper out on my lap.

I read.

I reread.

I closed the paper and handed it back to the man beside me.

Shocking, he said as he tucked the paper in the seat pocket in front of him, the words *Carry Dead Baby* just visible. Shocking, he said again, adding, Unbelievable what some people are capable of.

We talked quietly about the why of such a feat, not to mention the how, as the flight attendants made their dutiful announcements.

How could she not have known?

How could others not have known?

That night, as we sped through the dark clouds of time, flashes of this woman's life came to me in the glowing underlights of the airplane cabin.

There, on the floor of her New York hotel bathroom, she bore the hours of pain, and then the writhing and the struggle of something wrong, something horribly wrong, but something vital, something unstoppable, the heaving of her stomach, the clutching of the sink, so sure this could not happen, was not happening.

She had never felt pregnant.

She felt weird and large and strangely full but never pregnant.

The floor was cold beneath the porcelain sink of that dank hotel room as she pushed and strained, and felt her body trembling in pain. She pushed and she strained until all convulsions ceased, all movement and sound hushed, as if she were dropping into a wide, cool ocean that embraced every inch of her bare and blood-smeared skin, releasing her of all hurt, all fury and illness, all she did wrong, all she did right.

She looked down to see a tiny body, wet and lifeless but moveable and pink, a tiny face of sleep. Her fingers gingerly felt his small patch of hair and smoothed his wet skin, and for a few seconds, he reminded her of a plastic doll from her childhood.

She knew then that everything would change. But she had to do what was right, right? Had to take care of him. Had to carry him back to her mother, carry him back to England, where she would make it all okay again, where she would right all that she had wronged.

She tried to cry and held him tighter, his body curled and becoming more and more rigid as she pressed him near her bare skin. She looked for something to make him comfortable, warm. She pulled a damp towel down from the rail above, and she gently wrapped it around him, and she knew she could not cry, that the baby could not cry, that he would never cry.

She sat on the bathroom floor for hours that seemed like days, months, maybe years, until, finally, she pulled herself upright, stumbling a little as she stood.

How did it feel to wrap his body in the blanket pulled from the unmade bed, to see him lying there as you dressed and readied yourself to leave the hotel, this city, this mess, as you moved from the hotel doors to the busy streets, as you carried him near your chest in the jolting cab, along the long roads, and then to the ticket counter at the airport?

How did it feel to bring him through security, tightly wrapped and tightly held, as other parents messed with their bottles and diapers and toys and crying children?

At the gate, the airline staff suspected something was wrong with the unmoving bundle that the woman pressed against her chest.

Discreet phone calls were made, authorities alerted.

Police officers appeared.

You have the right to remain silent, they said, standing in front of her, in back of her.

And she did. And the baby did. And she did not cry as they pried him from her arms, when once he had slithered out, wet and lifeless but moveable and pink, a tiny face of sleep.

As the sky grew pink and the bustle of breakfast began, drowsy passengers rubbed their eyes, while children continued to sleep, weighted dolls of limp hands and small lips drawing breath in the unconscious knowledge that others will hold them, feed them, rock them to sleep, rock them awake, carry them home.

As the captain announced, Twenty minutes to go, folks, the man beside me asked, So what made her do it?

I shook my head. Insanity? Guilt? Maybe sadness?

I looked at my dry breakfast. Maybe love?

Mmm, the man said, taking a bite of his hard croissant, I'm not so sure there was any love there. Can't call it love if it's murder.

I felt the eager expectation of my children's small hands, and asked, But how could they know it was murder? Maybe she's more victim than perpetrator?

The passenger tapped the newsprint with his finger, folded back to the crossword. Got to trust the authorities on this one. They've already charged her. First degree.

But how could they know? I asked again.

I guess they feel if a woman is crazy enough to carry a dead baby on a plane, she's crazy enough to commit murder.

And yet if she—and the baby—had made it to England, she'd be in a hospital and not a prison. The British doctors are saying she's in desperate need of care. Under a great deal of psychological stress.

That's what they're saying. But who's to say who's right? One thing's for certain: the US authorities aren't going to let her go anywhere until they know for sure.

He sighed and went back to his crossword, filling squares with capital letters, nodding with satisfaction at the word *unrequited* as he took bites of a hard croissant.

But I knew that word didn't fit.

I leaned back in my seat as the plane began to descend, and I thought about my waiting children.

I thought about how their cries of hello would sound as I moved past passport control, past customs, past the opening doors into the long corridor of waiting faces, the corridor of friends and family who will be there, standing, smiling, eagerly anticipating the arrival of loved ones, and I knew which ones would be warm, real, mine.

I thought about how my children's warm bodies would feel as they burrowed themselves into my arms, as they took my hands in theirs, one on each side, as we moved together beyond Heathrow's terminal, past the glass doors, into a jolting cab, along the many humming roads leading toward home.

"The first line of this story presents a character, setting and situation with a rare and satisfying command of storytelling. Using perfect details balanced against rapid pacing, the voice of this writing has an air of stern and simple elegance, and reveals how the narrator's experience of a newspaper story becomes a parallel challenge to her own ambivalence about motherhood and love. In the way that great stories open larger questions, within its brief time frame this story questions culture and society, and how we are so quick and sure to judge the tragedies of others, yet with less capacity to examine the perils in our own judgments."—Eugenia Kim, Final Judge, 2015 Able Muse Write Prize (for fiction) on this winning story, "After Reading the News Story of a Woman Who Attempted to Carry Her Dead Baby onto an Airplane" by Andrea Witzke Slot.

ABLE MUSE WRITE PRIZE FOR POETRY, 2015 ▪ FINALIST

Jeanne Wagner

On Watching a *Cascade* Commercial

I've turned down the sound—so they float on my screen:
there she is, standing with a man in her kitchen, holding

out a goblet so clean the light loves it, casts its studied
gleam on the crystalline curve right above where

her fingers clasp the stem. I could say they look like
they found the grail, but that isn't the story here,

which is both irony and its opposite, a tale of the two
of them, radiant with newfound clarity—a domestic

triangle of material desire, which is a kind of love, its
object not the touch of a stranger's skin, as it often is,

not a child, but the generous shape of a thing whose
curve is an open globe, inviting them to place their lips

on its rim, to drink the uncontainable air. Refraction
is a gift of light, the aureole around the magic

comic book ring. Fair Isolde holding her cup, made safe
with its shine of compunction, its antidote of air.

ABLE MUSE WRITE PRIZE FOR POETRY, 2015 ▪ FINALIST

Elise Hempel

The Jockey

Atop his exhausted buggy with its
rusted wheels and now-stuck key,
one boot missing, a faded jersey,
the bill of his cap cracked off, he sits

behind a nicked brown horse that once
flicked its tail, clattered around
planked floor or rug when the buggy was wound
after school by children who've since

fallen behind him, white-haired or gone,
as he still waves the flopping spring
of his crop, still stares through dimming
goggles, gathering gray ribbons

of dust in his silent, frozen race
down an ever-unfurling track,
hunched to win, leaving far back
all claps and laughter, his once-smooth face

scarred and pitted, just the white
fleck of a smile now, more a sneer,
his empty fists on the reins of air
still holding tight.

ABLE MUSE WRITE PRIZE FOR POETRY, 2015 ▪ WINNER

Elise Hempel

Cathedral Peppersauce

I grasp its beauty now, this bottle once
a soldier grasped for need in the Civil War,
carried with razor, tin plate and cup, his guns
from camp to camp, this bottle he must have admired

if only for a moment, pulling it up
from his weathered bag each day, having to notice
the slender neck, blue glass, its globed lip
in his gaunt hold as he poured the sauce

over his meager meal; he must have seen
its six arched sides rising as the sauce waned,
its beveled windows, felt its raised design
of tiny flowers against his dusty hand

and paused at the little arched door before he ate
the rancid meat, marched back toward hell's gate.

"The formal qualities of 'Cathedral Peppersauce' are elegant: slant rhymes throughout, until the final couplet clicks the poem closed with a perfect rhyme. Even more elegant, though, is the poem's way of grasping the beauty of its subject, by looking simultaneously at the bottle and through it into history, from which it recuperates, through sympathy and particularity, a life lost long ago."—H.L. Hix, Final Judge, 2015 Able Muse Write Prize (for poetry) on this winning poem, "Cathedral Peppersauce" by Elise Hempel.

Stephen Kampa

Meeting David Foster Wallace for the First Time (Again)

A Review of David Foster Wallace, *Both Flesh and Not: Essays*
New York, NY: Little, Brown and Company, 2012
ISBN 9780316182386, 336 pp., USA $17.00, paperback

★ ★ ★

I find myself in the not-uncommon position—for me, anyway—of being a lover of books and language, a constant reader, and a self-proclaimed eclectic who has never read a particular major author: in this case, David Foster Wallace. I have reasons.

For one, I remember many years ago making the nearly obligatory attempt at *Infinite Jest* that any self-respecting literary aspirant then made, and I never got past the hundredth page. I recall almost nothing specific from the novel—with the exception of one detail I now find snortingly funny, that years had finally been sold for advertising, so that instead of calling a year "2013," say, characters would call it "The Year of the Depends Undergarment"—but I do remember my general impressions and the way they kept me from continuing. Too much faux (and faux-faux) pedantry, those exasperating footnotes, the impossible plot (wait, there was a plot?), and worst of all, the sense that the author was not only playing a game—as all writers do, whether they're honest about that or not—but that he also wanted me to see it at every turn, wanted me to watch myself be meta-manipulated in an act of auto-voyeurism. I imagined him as a magician who patiently, superciliously explains his trick while he's performing it, so that you're most amazed by the fact that you still feel a little fooled by his legerdemain until he says, "Let me turn that around so you can *really* see how it works."

For another, it seemed like the sort of reader (or, more often, writer) who embraced Wallace was not only the sort of reader/writer with whom I rarely agreed, but also the sort of *person* with whom I rarely wanted to spend time. You know, the same guy (why were they so often men?) who would relentlessly drop the names of obscure bands, bands whose reputations derived from their novel instrumentation: handmade pizza-box dulcimer, sampled Gameboy theme songs, didgeridoo, and stationary bicycle. Jaded. All their comedy self-vaunting. Never good with relationships.

I think, though, most of my resistance arose from the suspicion that Mr. Wallace was playing literary games with no real stakes; that is to say, I was afraid he had no heart. Even if all writing requires that writers play games—everything from simple chess-like problems of plot to the anagrams and acrostics of a George Herbert or a Nabokov—I back away from books where I sense that winning or losing the game would have no effect on either writer or reader. (Games can have massive stakes; they can even be dangerous. Think Russian roulette.) I could not tell from the little I read whether Mr. Wallace *believed* in anything, or at least felt bereft at the lack of a belief-object, and that meant to me that I didn't need to keep reading. I am happily afflicted with the conviction that great art has, at its very roots, not artistic concerns but human ones.

So, oddly enough, when I was looking at the library for something to read once I felt done reading for the day—something I could read without being heavily *invested*—I picked up *Both Flesh and Not* by David Foster Wallace. Essays, I thought, meant less commitment—I wouldn't be swept up by narrative momentum (wait, there was a plot?)—and an author that I didn't like meant I could pay less attention. Sort of a beach read, if your beach happened to be a wrinkled gray-brown couch. With beer handy. Or beers.

I was most surprised to find Mr. Wallace *companionable*—hardly the heartless aesthete I'd inferred him to be, but rather the sort of person I'd want to sit down with at the pub after a long day of teaching and talk about (not necessarily in this order) (a) life, (b) art, (c) words, (d) teaching, (e) necessary kung fu films, (f) unnecessary poets, (g) what happens when you die, and (h) why it matters if we love at all. I should have known from the brief "Publisher's Note" at the beginning of the collection that this would be the case—it states, after all, that Wallace "possessed an insatiable love for words and their meanings" and that he "constantly updated a list of words that he wanted to learn," and as proof of this excerpts from said list interleave the essays in a surprisingly touching display of one writer's devotion to what always comes first and foremost, his native language. But, partway through his first essay I stopped, put down the book, and started writing the first three paragraphs of this piece. I wanted to get down my prejudices intact because I knew they weren't going to survive the reading of the whole thing.

I found myself interested in things that do not interest me—tennis, for example, which is what two of the essays (including that first) are about—and Wallace sent me not just back to books I'd ignored or to books I'd never heard of, but in a passionately argued analysis of "F/X Porn," he convinced me I needed to see *The Terminator* and *Alien,* two films I'd blown off for years. His voice ranges from the astonishingly, obviously intelligent to the intimately colloquial, and his perceptions about writing—the act, the life, the biz—are bold and at times prescient.

In "Fictional Futures and the Conspicuously Young," for example, he does a laudable job of identifying three things that distinguish the young writers at hand from predecessors: "the impacts of television, of academic creative writing programs, and of a revolution in the way educated people understand the function and possibility of literary narrative." He analyzes the first so well that it almost seems prophetic of reality television culture:

> Think, for instance, about the way prolonged exposure to broadcast drama makes each one of us at once more self-conscious and less reflective. A culture more and more about *seeing* eventually perverts the relation of seer and seen . . . We, the audience, receive unconscious reinforcement of the thesis that the most significant feature of persons is *watchableness,* and that contemporary human worth is not just isomorphic with but rooted in the phenomenon of watching. Precious distinctions between truly being and merely appearing get obfuscated.

I could forgive that "isomorphic" because of the exciting precision of the argument here. He continues:

> Then consider that well-known, large, "ignorant" segment of the population that believes on a day-to-day level that what happens on televised dramas is "real." This, the enormous volume of mail addressed each day to characters and not the persons who portray them, is the iceberg's extreme tip. The berg itself is a generation (New) for whom the distinction between (real) actor artificially portraying and (pretend) character genuinely behaving gets ever more tangled. The danger of the berg is badness and cost—a shift from an understanding of self as a character in a great drama whose end is meaning to an understanding of self as an actor at a great audition whose end is *seeming,* i.e., being seen.

If I've quoted at length, it's because from here it's about a half-hour to *Jersey Shore,* where the *only* virtue may be not *watchableness* but *watchedness.* Moreover, if you doubt the validity of the argument having larger social ramifications, I would challenge you to remember any of the times you've seen a young member of the family—a sibling, child, younger cousin, niece or nephew, grandchild, whatever—scrolling on an iPhone through pictures or videos of more watchable moments than the family gathering they're currently attending. As if that little bit of minor prophesying weren't enough, the essay also includes a lacerating evaluation of creative writing programs, one that I suspect has only become more valid in the intervening decades. My favorite image in the essay—and one of my favorites in the book—comes from this section, where Wallace lists as one of the obvious dangers "faculty power struggles that summon images of sharks fighting for control of a bathtub."

That sense of humor—from tickling to gut-socking, bemused to defiant—everywhere, finds expression. Wallace has a way with phrasing and few fears: "As of 2003," he writes in "Twenty-Four Word Notes," "misusing *that* for *who* or *whom*, whether in writing or speech, functions as a kind of class-marker—it's the grammatical equivalent of wearing NASCAR paraphernalia or liking pro wrestling." Not watching; *liking*. But he also builds comedy into the very form of some of these pieces, which can then set him up for even more effective one-liners. His review of *The Best of The Prose Poem* begins

- Physical dimensions of *The Best of The Prose Poem: An Inter-national Journal* anthology in cm: 15 x 22.5 x 2.
- Weight of anthology in grams: 419.
- Total # of words in anthology: 85, 667.
- Total # of words devoted to actual prose poems: 69,986.
- *Rain Taxi*'s length-limit for review of *Best of The P.P.*: 1,000 words.

and includes this item a few lines down

- Tactical reason for review form: The words preceding each item's colon technically constitute neither subjective complement nor appositive nor really any recognized grammatical unit at all; hence none of these antecolonic words should count against *R.T.*'s rigid 1,000-word limit.

and then adds, in case you've missed one of the jokes:

- Other, better-known and/or currently fashionable transgeneric literary forms: the Nonfiction Novel, the Prose Poem, the Lyric Essay, etc.

All well and good, and the piece has as a virtue not just its I'll-get-the-better-of-The-Man gamesmanship, but also its sound critical sense: when Wallace adduces an example of flabby, clunky, or bad writing, you are guaranteed it will be flabby, clunky, or bad. (It's easy to forget how rare that can be in a review.) But the coup de grâce for me, the laugh-out-loud one-liner that I didn't see coming throughout the review—no matter how often the anthology editor's name was mentioned—was this one:

- Probability that, if this reviewer were named Peter Johnson, he would publish under "Pete" or his first two initials: 100%.

Even retyping that *ad nominem* attack, I laughed until there were tears in my eyes.

I need to spend just a bit more time on critical sensibility. Despite being billed as an experimentalist, Wallace more than once surprised me with a formulation that seemed to me entirely traditional; yet he derives from these dicta techniques and ideas that lead him (in the little fictive snippet I read so long ago, or even in the way he tackles the nonfiction forms here) in interesting, unexpected directions. In the same prose-poem anthology review, itself so unorthodox, he writes in a footnote,

> In regarding formal conventions primarily as "rules" to rebel against, the Professional Transgressor fails to see that conventions often *become* conventions precisely because of their power and utility, i.e., because of the paradoxical freedoms they permit the artist who understands how to use (not merely "obey") them.

And as mentioned above, his sensibility is discerning to the point of being seemingly infallible: when he critiques the language of two "Math Melodrama" novels, he zeroes in on precisely those sentences that best exemplify the fact that the work of translation should have been delegated to someone other than the novels' respective ("semi-bilingual") authors. Not every reviewer does this. When I read poetry reviews, I am sometimes astonished at the banality of lines that a reviewer has quoted as an example of so-and-so's lyricism, and I will never, never forgive the incompetent reviewer who presented two perfectly scannable—indeed, rhythmically nuanced—lines of verse as evidence of a great poet's inability to handle meter. Furthermore, some reviewers or critics whom I suspect of being able to do justice (whatever that might look like) to a work often refuse to do so, most likely for political, personal, or careerist reasons. It makes one all the more grateful to read prose by someone who is able and willing to call the good good and the bad bad.

In this, Wallace reminds me, oddly enough, of Randall Jarrell, who rhapsodizes of what he loves and excoriates what he hates; there is in Wallace that same utter devotion to what he thinks marvelous and the same foregone-conclusion dismissiveness to what he thinks is dreck. In this book, at least, there are ample discussions of both. (Here it might be worth noting that one reason I cannot trust William Logan—and think him no fit inheritor of the mantle of Jarrell, no matter how obviously he models himself on that great writer—is that while he is as unsparing as Jarrell was of the mediocre, he appears to have no great enthusiasms. Jarrell, it should be noted, *gushed* when he loved something—gushed to the point even of slight embarrassment on his behalf—and whether that made his prose more elegant or not, it certainly made his judgment more reliable. One never suspected him of a pandemic animus.) If Wallace thinks that *The Terminator* was "one of the two best US action movies of the entire 1980s" and "a dark, breathlessly kinetic, near-brilliant piece of metaphysical Ludditism," he'll tell you so; conversely, if he thinks *Terminator 2: Judgment Day* is "empty and derivative, pure mimetic polycelluloid," he'll tell you that, too.

Now, in my book, to spend this much time praising an author without acknowledging his foibles is the microcosmic version of the all-or-nothing critical stance decried above, and Wallace does have foibles. Foremost are his mannerisms, everything from the incessant footnotes (like a child interrupting a conversation every three or four sentences) to the overabundance of abbreviations, including nonce ones. Perhaps to a lesser degree, as is to be expected of a writer with such impressive intellectual gifts, Wallace occasionally indulges in unendearing displays of learning; put simply, he shows off, and in those moments, he reminds me of the precocious undergrad everyone wishes would graduate already and move on to the Real World where someone with back hair will teach him a lesson about showing off. It's not a generous impulse on everyone's part, but there it is. To be honest, though, as I have come to terms with the fact that there are far more people than I'd ever realized who are much, much smarter than I am, I feel less threatened by these intellectual barrel rolls and loop-de-loops. Wallace is curious, and he satisfies his curiosity by learning, and after he's learned something he longs to share it; if that lovely propensity occasionally manifests its obnoxious side, I'm glad to take the bad with the good.

In reading this collection of essays, I met a writer who could panegyrize dogs and kraut (". . . but then you find out they're really long and *really* good, and that the kraut is the really smelly gloppy kind that's revolting when you're not in the mood for kraut but rapturously yummy when you are in the mood") as easily as he celebrated a novel that was "a dramatic rendering of what it would be like to live in the sort of universe described by logical atomism"; who could meditate seriously on the "erotic malaise of the '70s" and affirm "real sexuality is about our struggles to connect with one another, to erect bridges across the chasms that separate selves" and conclude, "Sexuality is, finally, about *imagination*"; who could criticize American consumer culture even as he used it as a wellspring for comedy; and who felt the pressing political pressures of the last years of his life as an impetus for imagining—again, that belief in the power of imagination—what the future might bring.

The book's title, *Both Flesh and Not*, comes from the first essay, "Federer Both Flesh and Not," and that title from a description within the essay of the eponymous tennis great: ". . . he looks like what he may well (I think) be: a creature whose body is both flesh and, somehow, light"; but the title also reminds us of the hope of any writer to be both a body of blood and bones and a body of work, and it is surely every writer's hope that the latter will survive long after the former is gone. I believe the best writers know somewhere within that this kind of immortality is, at best and worst, irrelevant: at best, if one survives death and enters into something else, one's body of work will likely mean little there, and at worst, if one's consciousness simply ends at the moment of death, a body of work will mean less than nothing to the person who created it. So much for immortality. Why write, then? Why hope that the not-flesh body survives? It has to do, I think, with the deep realization that we are gifts to each other in *both* bodies—gifts of wisdom, at times, but more often gifts of companionship and laughter, gifts of shared grief and hope—and that the body we leave behind, the body of work, can continue to be a gift long after the fleshly one has been fully given. Judging by this book, Mr. Wallace's body of work is indisputably such a gift.

Léon Leijdekkers

FEATURED ARTIST

Léon Leijdekkers
A Photographic Exhibit

Léon Leijdekkers was born in 1962 in Zierikzee, the Netherlands. In his self-described colorful memory, he mainly spent his youth wandering through nature on the beautiful island of Schouwen-Duiveland. It's then that he started taking pictures and got his own darkroom. A professional career as a classical musician and later in orchestra management forced him to move and live elsewhere and in the process he lost his connection with photography, albeit not entirely. He recently discovered the world of digital photography and became very inspired by this new form. Léon attended master classes in Yorkshire, England, with the great photographer Martin Henson. Later he specialized in long-exposure photography with Jonathan Chritchley in French Basque country. And recently he joined Bill Schwab on a tour of the Faroe Islands—an inspiring journey with one of the truly great masters of modern photography. He owes these men, he says, and so many others a great deal of gratitude for inspiring him. But most inspiration, now and back then in his younger years, derives from the works of Beethoven, Schubert, Shostakovich, Webern and Ravel, and others. Without their music, he reckons this world would be a much, much darker place.

★★★

Featured Art
from Léon Leijdekkers
★ ★ ★

Artist Statement

I am a Dutch fine-art photographer and trained classical musician. My photography can be described as a lifelong journey to the lost sense of connectivity of youth, when knowledge, intellect and responsibilities did not yet pose a barrier between the surrounding natural world and the inner core. My tool is a camera. My self-imposed boundaries are square format, monochrome and long-exposure photography. My subject matter is scenery, often seascapes—in essence indescribable but a gut punch, and evoking the feeling of connectivity like a late piano sonata by Beethoven or a string quartet by Shostakovich, which is music consoling in a sense that makes one realize we are kindred spirits in this world. The resulting photographs aim to communicate this notion.

More artwork, biographical information, news and updates can be found at my website, www.monochromejourneys.com.

★★★

Featured Art
from Léon Leijdekkers
★ ★ ★

Abbey Light

Abbaye de Fontenay, France, July 2010

Church Rock, Study #2

COMMODIOUS SACRAMENT

Elegug Stacks, Pembrokeshire, Wales

CONNEMARA

Derryclare, Lough, Ireland, August 2013

Derelict Dream

Wierum, the Netherlands, August 2011

HOMAGE TO MARTIN HENSON

Portbail, Normandy, France, December 2009

L'Île du Guesclin

Bretagne, France, February 2010

Journey to No End

Llyn y Dywarchen, Wales, August 2012

LES BRAVES

Monument on Omaha Beach, Normandy, France

LIGHTHOUSE

Westkapelle, the Netherlands, October 2009

The Cloister, One Late Afternoon

Mont Saint-Michel, Normandy, France, February 2008

In the Crypt #3

Mont Saint-Michel, Normandy, France, February 2010

Oosterscheldekering, Study #3

Zeeland, the Netherlands, July 2014

Pentre Ifan, Study #1

Newport, Wales, February 2014

L'abbaye de Pontigny

Pontigny, France, July 2010

Risin og Kellingin

Tjørnuvík, Streymoy, Faroe Islands, April 2013

Sanctuary

Santiago de Compostela, Spain, April 2011

Sea Wall

Port Racine, Normandy, France, December 2009

Secluded Confidence

Mont Saint-Michel, Normandy, France, December 2010

THE CURVE

Saint-Vaast-La-Hougue, France, December 2009

FICTION

Paul Soto
Polaroid

The boy found the stick at the edge of a creek between his street and the woods and knew from the way it stood, smooth and straight in the grainy mush, that it was special. It had not been there the day before. The boy stood behind the picket fence of the Braun Street ghost house and watched the old swing rock into a lull. The house, glazed over by a bleak, country orange looked out into the settling afternoon and offered no remarks.

He whistled the beginning of his favorite song again and again, starting over if he missed any notes. It was a glad little tune, and although he did not know its name he always asked his father to play it on mornings before school. He spun the stick in his hand. The boy hoped to bless it with bathwater and a prayer once he got home.

The boy looked back from the fence and towards Edwin's front door, hoping he would not see him rumble out of his house and onto the street. Today he had taken the far sidewalk and run past Edwin's house, eyes on the concrete. Edwin's parents let him drink Coca-Cola for breakfast and play in the rain, and the boy did not understand how Edwin's mother never called him in for dinner or drove him to school. The day before Edwin had been outside in his yard, poking at ant piles with a pencil. The boy had wanted to show someone the dam by the river, and although Edwin was a little mean, he was strong enough to carry some bigger rocks that the dam still needed.

They hopped over a root and onto a grave of leaves. Snapping a weed under his foot, the boy cleared a branch from his face and pointed at the timid stream whispering between the rocks. Edwin stumbled behind him and made a horrible noise, like an angry vacuum cleaner, and stomped his foot into the mush.

"You said it was a river!"

The boy didn't understand. It *was* a river. There was flowing water and dragonflies and, on sunnier days, the tadpoles shot out of the moss and nibbled on the floating leaves. It didn't have to be big to be a river. As long as there was life in it and it was deep enough to walk into, it was a river.

"What's that?"

Edwin pointed at a small dam in the stream that rose neatly over a glassy, bronze puddle. The boy had spent a whole Saturday picking out the smoothest stones in the woods. He found crickets and worms under the stones and promised to make them a great lake in return. He found the best branches around a log and alongside them, hundreds of gray, spindly urchins that had fallen from the trees. The boy took his things to the base of the stream and built his dam for all the tadpoles and dragonflies and leaves and, maybe one day, even real fish. He had come to visit it for the past two days and watched the trees above him waver on the surface.

"That's my dam."

"I'm gonna tell my mom you said that!"

"What?"

"You're lucky I'm your friend."

Edwin ran to the edge of the stream and stood over the dam. He studied his face and leaned over to see if he could find anything else. Then, scraping his breath, he spat out a pale, foamy glob.

"Hey!" The boy stood in his place, hands crawling towards his pockets. "Stop! Please. Please stop!" Edwin laughed and spat again. The boy watched the spit spin and spread through the water.

The boy balanced himself on his toes and peered over the picket fence and into the yard. The swing whined for him. He planted his elbows between the spades and studied the swing's slow, perfect movement. It reminded him of his father's breaths when he'd nap on Sundays after lunch, with an issue of *Time* magazine rising and sighing over his chest. A crow dropped onto the yard, scanned, and left hastily.

The peeling old house did not intimidate the boy as it did his friends. It summoned in him a vague feeling of home, as if he had lived there before and had taken baths and eaten soup there. He could imagine its familiar smell although he could not find any wisp of it in his memory. The house had become the focus of his bike rides around the neighborhood since last Halloween, when his mother sharpened her pace past its chipped and sullen fences. Its windows whispered secrets to him and although he could not express them, even to himself, he cherished the private colors that they ignited within him.

The next night, after asking his mother about the house, she took a few breaths and placed her hands on his chest.

"Not all families love each other. Sometimes they treat each other badly." She grazed through the roots of his hair.

"How?"

She pressed her hand over his hair and pushed it down, sliding her hand back to his neck.

"Some families just don't love each other."

"But why?"

The boy's mother sighed and leaned away, dropping her hands to her lap.

"Your Popo was their dentist so he knew them well. He gave the girls their braces and fixed their cavities." She kissed the boy's forehead. "But their daddy drank very much. When you're a grown up it's okay to drink grown-up drinks—but only a little bit. Their daddy drank very much and would get angry at the mommy and the girls for no reason."

The boy sat up against the headboard.

"Then they all stopped going to church and no one from the neighborhood really saw them anymore. One of the daughters put her things into a backpack and ran away one morning and no one ever saw her again. And one day their daddy drank a lot and fell asleep in his car and almost hit another car but ended up falling into a little canal off the side of the road. After that the mommy was very upset and she left with the other daughter for another town far away." She kissed the boy's forehead again.

"And the daddy?"

The boy's mother opened her mouth and said nothing. She squeezed his palm and kissed his knuckles. She smiled but the boy knew that smiles were only real when people smiled with their eyes. Her eyes looked worried. He held her hand tighter.

"What happened to the daddy?"

The boy's mother smiled again without her eyes and placed her hand over the boy's chest.

"Their daddy stayed in the house and kept drinking. And one day his body could not take any more drinking so he passed away."

"By himself? In that house?"

She looked over him and into the headboard.

"Yes, sweetheart. But that's only—"

"He died all alone?"

"Yes, but that's why it's important for families to love and take care of each other, so we can be there . . ."

Her voice began to float away and blend with the whir of the fan. The boy felt heavy in his insides, as if he had just swallowed a cloud. He imagined the father's ghost, all alone in that house, floating among the rooms, wailing for his family to finally come back. He could see him tired and crying, checking his watch and looking out the window like his mother would when his cousins came over for Easter.

"Sweetheart, you know I would never let that happen to you. You know that, right?"

Her eyes sharpened, like she had just seen a killer clown.

"Do you understand, honey? I would never, ever let that happen to you, or your father, or anyone else. This just happens when families don't love each other. You trust me, don't you?"

The boy nodded again, confused by the glaze over her eyes. He knew that he would be okay and that his mother would always love him, even if he died one day. He also knew that the ghost in the house would be okay and that one day the family would come back and the ghost would go back to being a person and the grass in their yard would come back, too. But the boy didn't know why his mother's grip trembled over his own and why her breath shook through her gown and into the bed. The boy thought that heartbeats made people real, but now, in the dry, distended moonlight, his mother's heartbeat frightened him and he wished it would slow down. Hurriedly the boy kissed her hand.

"I love you, sweetheart."

The boy felt like his river when his mother said she loved him. He loved his mother and had wished to marry her until his father laughed and patted his back, telling him that he would have to find a pretty girl of his own to marry. But the boy wanted to feel like a river and when his mother passed by to say good night was when he felt most real, like his spirit slept the whole day and only then rose to burn through his fingers as he played with her hair as she leaned over him. But the way his mother spoke now worried him as she lay next to him, her hair flooding over his chest.

"You know that your guardian angel is always there for you, right?" He could feel her heartbeat knocking on his belly. Maybe her heartbeat was looking for his.

The boy nodded and kissed her head, hoping that she would feel better. If he kissed her and held her hand she would be okay again. He asked about the daughter who ran away, and she said that she did not know her well. The daughter was much older and went to the high school, but was known for wandering the trails behind the neighborhood and playing her guitar in the yard, singing for the neighbors and the dogs. His mother said that her voice was the best in the church choir and that she was very pretty and had hair like a mermaid. He loved reading about mermaids and hoped to take to the sea one day when he was old as his father and find one to marry.

His mother's sleeping breaths whistled toward the moonlight as he wove through her hair. Her arm slung over him and dangled over the edge of the bed. The boy thought that his mother was the prettiest girl in the world. He loved her hair and her face and the way she loved him. But the boy kept wondering about the mermaid girl and her guitar and imagined that she never wore shoes and that she was out somewhere in the night, maybe even in the woods, walking barefoot across his river. The boy counted his mother's breaths and thought of the mermaid girl until she appeared to him, singing.

He imagined her skin glowing in the darkness and that they'd kneel together to pray a Hail Mary every night. For weeks she'd take him to the ocean when his parents fell asleep and they'd swim and see dolphins and coral and all the other mermaids with soft voices. She'd teach him how to breathe underwater and talk to fish, and once the moon sank in the sky, he'd take her back home and hide her in the bathtub where she would wait until he returned from school.

He made many names for her and changed the color of her eyes and drew her in the back of his old notebook so no one else could ever find her. He felt her living in him when he was at school and at the grocery store until, after Christmas, he had forgotten her song.

The boy, touching the gaps between the fence posts, felt that this house was more of a home than his own. The yard was wild in a way his was not. The boy felt this in the space between his stomach and his heart, where he imagined the cove of his soul. Thumping his belly with the magic stick, he opened the chipped gate and entered the yard.

The tree on which the swing hung was strong and gorgeous. Its branches looked like the arms of God. He looked up into the twining wood, making out shapes and words like "why." His neck began to hurt and he looked again in front of him, approaching the creaky swing as if it were a sleeping wolf. He reached for the worn chain and caressed it carefully. The rust nibbled at his fingers. He gripped the chain and pulled. The swing wobbled and stayed in place, squealing frailly. Exhaling, he sat on the swing and let the breeze push him toward the house. He pointed the stick up and closed his eyes.

The house held itself upon a worn gray patio, the color of a summer day hesitating to rain. Several isles of peeled wood lay scattered across the patio. The door, guarded by decrepit, uneven columns, was battered and its hinges bent. Even if it was open, the boy had a bad feeling about going through it, for he was sure he'd find a killer clown or maybe even the lonely ghost. The boy hopped off the swing and headed towards the backyard holding his stick like a sword. His palms began to sweat.

The sky was sliding into a thick, bloody pink, dripping its tired hue over the remains of the back garden. Between the clumps of dirt lay a few scattered cactuses. The boy squatted to examine the dusty soil, sifting with the stick for new stems or seeds. Finding nothing, he held his palm steady over one of the cactuses, a stout, proud plant, hovering just enough to avoid a prick. He walked through the weeds, hearing the first crickets chirp near him. A tennis ball lay cracked and gray, nestled between several tufts of wild grass. He left it as it was. The boy followed the patio to the back of the house. One of the windows hung open, revealing an incredible darkness. His heart rolled down like a ball towards a gutter. He dragged his hand over his shirt and gripped the stick with the other.

Although the window scared the boy, the secret feelings that the house whispered slowed his heart. The stick would guide him and keep him safe. The house made him feel in ways only his mother's voice would when she sang to him or when he would thank God and the Angels for so many things at once that he felt full and no longer human. The boy knelt into the grass, kissed his stick, and stepped towards the open window.

The glass on the window was riddled with dust. He impaled the dark with his stick that he swung between the frames and into the house. Feeling nothing, the boy climbed onto the sill and slid over, tapping the floor with his magic stick.

The house smelled of forgotten fruit and of the old library by the town plaza. The boy trudged through the darkness and the odor, following a single, tepid stream of light. There was not much daylight left now and the boy's mother would be out looking for him at any moment.

Chairs without tables were strewn throughout the house. A box holding a hump of clothes sat tucked into a dark corner. A floorboard screeched at the boy and he jumped, nearly dropping his stick into the murk.

In the dark, the fireplace looked like a face. The boy wondered if that was where the old ghost waited and whether it was he who left the window open for the boy. The boy poked inside the hearth. The ash smelled like Thanksgiving and, closing his eyes, he imagined the ghost and his family having a big dinner together and eating lots of mashed potatoes.

The ceiling rose and folded above him, high like the one at the movie theater. He felt safe in the house now and was sure that if there were a ghost, he would be nice and happy to have a visitor. If the ghost really missed his family he could use the boy's stick to bring them back. All he had to do was kiss it and whisper his wish and his family would come back right away. The boy would just find another one at the creek tomorrow, and maybe one day he'd come back to see if the ghost had used it. He spun a circle with the stick, brought it to his chest, and set it on the floor.

The boy looked back at the open window, watching the light thin and recede into the yard. It wouldn't be long until dark. He stepped towards the window, keeping his eyes on the stairs. Whatever flowed from the house, the boy felt that it came from upstairs.

He ran up and, expecting to fall through the loose floorboards, leapt onto the second floor, stumbling onto a musty red rug. The boy stood up and followed it, passing the empty rooms and walls. He turned into a dead end—an empty bookshelf stood against the wall like a thick scab. He approached the bookshelf and ran his hands through it, even though he could now see that it held nothing for him. He skimmed the surface of the three shelves twice. He felt something in the right corner of the bottom shelf.

He drew it out carefully and rushed to the closest window. Turning it under the ebbing light, the boy squinted into his palm. It was a piece of yellowed, brittle paper, faded under various smudges of muck and, elegant and swooping in the bottom corner, "Tamalpais, 1973." Tenderly pinching the top of the paper, he flipped it over. The boy's soul swung.

It was a picture of a young woman, and immediately the boy knew that he loved her. She stood at the edge of a lake under a morning sun. She wore jeans and a sand-colored shirt etched with vines and petals. The boy turned the picture, hoping to somehow see the shape of her feet. Her collarbones curved and melted into her warm shoulders, her neck hiding half of itself in the flow of her mermaid hair. Her brows stood thick and woven like his mother's and her eyes, ardent and hazel, looked out of the picture and into the boy as if she knew that the photograph was for him to find.

The boy loved her and fought to remember her name. The picture crackled in his hands as he stared back into her face, attempting to recall her name, her voice, her song, and embarrassed by the sudden awareness of his actions and thoughts, the boy descended swiftly into numbness, only to surge again at the sight of her face. Her name hung on his tongue like a forgotten prayer and he could not find the strength to muster through to it.

The light was almost gone now and the thought of curfew dug into the boy's heart. He imagined marrying the girl by their river in the woods and pictured his lips on her forehead. He imagined the joy of tangling his fingers in her hair and the prospect of her forgotten name. He kissed the photograph.

The boy's mother called him from the street. Swallowing, he galloped down the stairs. He hurdled through the open window and hustled out of the yard, nearly tripping into the wild grass and its million singing crickets. He heard his mother call again. He ran forward and stopped under a street lamp and glimpsed the girl once more. Bringing the photograph back to the cove that could no longer hold his soul, he ran towards his mother at the end of the street, burning through the asphalt night. He had remembered her name.

Amit Majmudar

FEATURED POET

Amit Majmudar
Interviewed by Daniel Brown

Amit Majmudar is a widely published poet, novelist, and essayist whose next book *Dothead,* is forthcoming from Alfred A. Knopf in March 2016. More information is available at www.amitmajmudar.com.

◊ ◊ ◊ ◊

DB: You were raised in Cleveland, and the diction (and plenty of the matter) of your poems is as American as all get-out, but I'm going to stick my neck out and say that at least your paternal heritage seems Indian. I imagine a kid brought up essentially Midwestern, but in a family rich in Indian heritage. Have I got this right?

AM: Actually, I'm of Hindu Indian heritage on both sides. I was born in New York City, but my family moved to a small town called West Union, Ohio, when I was six months old or so. We stayed there for a bit, then moved to a suburb of Cleveland, where my first memories take place. I did second and third grade in Ahmedabad, India, when my family tried to relocate, but that didn't work out—we came right back to Cleveland. So except for that interlude, I've spent my whole life in Ohio—most of it within a 2.5-hour radius of Cleveland, college and medical training included.

DB: The basal Americanness of your poetry incorporates a fair amount of Indian (especially Hindu) matter. How do you tend to see the American and Indian sides of your poetry in relation to one another? Held in (fruitful) tension? Fused into a third thing? Some other way? Or maybe you're too busy producing—which you do a head-spinning amount of!—to give the matter much thought.

AM: You're right, I don't think about it much. Long ago I explained it, justified it, in terms of hybrid vigor—the idea, borrowed from genetics, that the crossbreed is inherently hardier. So I always regard hybridity, in myself or anyone else, as a good thing. (Whenever I do regard it, that is, which is only when other people ask me about it in interviews.)

In any case, I see myself, *literarily,* as an Old European. Almost all of my major influences, as I can discern them, are Continental or British. As a poet I was built by Shakespeare, Ovid, Goethe, Ariosto, Milton. You can see perhaps why my favorite living critic is George Steiner. My soul is Hindu, and my language is American. But in between the core and the surface there's a layer of solid Old Europe. It got in there at a very formative stage, when I was first discovering literature, and now it's there for good.

DB: Your blog (in the *Kenyon Review*) and essays provide an intriguing window into your poetics. A couple of key points I've ferreted out of these writings are a belief that lying is vital to poetry (*vis,* "the truest poetry is the most feigning"), and that the art as practiced today could use a good dose of the supernatural. These views seem related to me (they perhaps could be characterized jointly as an openness—or more—to the contrafactual). When and how did you come to them? Were certain poets influential in their formation?

AM: I think those need to be separated. The idea of the truest poets being the best liars is an old one—goes back to the Greeks. Today everyone values "authentic" poetry, a sense that the poet *really lived this anguish.* It's this demand that limits poets: one wishes that contemporary poetry readers set their poets free to lie. Laura likely didn't exist; Shakespeare wasn't a Danish prince; Ariosto wasn't a knight. I like the novel because the focus can shift away from the writer. One needn't endlessly elegize one's dead brother. Or imagine a dead brother for elegaic purposes.

I generally try to avoid writing about What It's Like To Be Indian In America, though it's always those kinds of poems that play the best; the title poem of my next book, after all, is *Dothead.*

As for the *supernatural,* it's catnip to the Muse and catnip to the masses. Witness the Ghost in what is definitely *not* a semi-autobiographical exploration of Shakespeare's Danish identity. Witness also the mythological or religious underpinnings of everything worth reading, right up until the rise of the nineteenth-century realist novel. (Which, curiously enough, is dominated by a Christian anarchist Russian, and an Irishman who reworked Homer.)

The question that relates these two ideas is this: Do you have to *believe* in the truth of the God or myth to write it truthfully, beautifully? I wager the answer is no: literal belief is not required by the Muse. So I don't believe Ovid literally believed in the myths of transformation he recounted in *Metamorphoses*. Creatively, there's probably a hybrid psychological state that defies the easy, binary characterization of belief or nonbelief. I don't think Dante thought Hell or Purgatory or Paradise "really" looked like his *Commedia* says they do. He believed the places existed hard enough to make up elaborate descriptions of them. And that is what is demanded of a poet. You must believe in something hard enough (*just* hard enough) to lie about it. "Beauty is truth," said the author of *Endymion*.

DB: So I guess I feel compelled to ask (against my better judgment, perhaps—and please feel free to demur): How might you position your above-mentioned "Hindu soul" in relation to belief, literal or literary? (In one of your poems you—or, er, the speaker—says, a bit grinningly but also perfectly seriously I think, "I'm not religious, Lord knows.")

AM: I think of religions as spiritual languages. A thinker can be fluent in Christianity and Islam and atheism—and may be able to travel, perhaps even pass as a native, in those intellectual lands—but no matter how spiritually cosmopolitan, a soul has only one mother tongue. I have written "Islamic" works (the novella/prose-poem *Azazil*, "The Autobiography of Khwaja Mustasim" from *Dothead*) and I have written "Judaeo-Christian" works (journals like *America*, *First Things*, and *Image* were among my earliest and most consistent publishers). But my mother tongue is Hinduism. And just as knowing Latin can help you pick up the Romance languages, Hinduism's poly/mono/theistic tradition (it's complicated, beyond the scope of this interview) has made learning, and writing in, other spiritual languages easy and pleasurable. Because where all Gods are simultaneously one God, and all earthly creatures are simultaneously divine, there can be no "other." Having Hinduism for my spiritual mother tongue has made every spiritual language my mother tongue. I am a foreigner nowhere.

DB: Jeez (said the Jew), am I glad I *did* ask that question; marvelous response. Your fluency in multiple religions calls to mind a corresponding plurality in your poetic persona, as you take on identities from different places and times. Most prominent in this regard is your recurring assumption of a middle-eastern guise. The poem "T.S.A." in *Dothead* suggests at least a partial basis for this affinity in recounting your being regularly mistaken for a middle easterner by airport screeners (and in referring to actual middle easterners singled out in this way as "my fellow 'Ahmeds'"). Is there anything to this connection?

AM: For sure. The great irony after 9/11 is that one of the few documented victims of a retaliatory hate crime was a Sikh—that is, a man who hailed from a religion that arose to combat Muslim hegemony in the Punjab, and whose ancient martyrs died at the hands of Muslim oppressors. It was a case of mistaken identity: a turbaned subcontinental man confused with the historic oppressor of his people. The old antagonisms mean even less than nothing on this side of the world; we are all "dark unshaven brothers," to quote the poem "T.S.A." In contemporary America, there *is* no "Hindu," "Muslim," "Sikh," no polytheistic idolator, no monotheistic iconoclast. The people who will suspect me—like, say, my pals over at Tampa International Airport this summer—suspect me without such trivial distinctions.

As for "fellow Ahmeds," my first name rhymes with "summit." Before 9/11, patients misheard my name as *Awm*it, or Uh-*meet*. After 9/11—like, literally on 9/12/01—the only way they misheard it was "Ahmed." They had Islam on the brain, as it were.

But this identity-switching, poetically, has a metaphysical basis. I believe that if I can include, in my inner pantheon, the most exclusivist One God—if I can incorporate and inhabit this diametrically opposite metaphysical system—then I will have radicalized, and perfected, my polytheism. *Dothead* enacts the well-documented syncretic tendency of Hinduism, giving it poetic form. The metaphysician and the physicist in me are both in search of the unified field.

DB: There are a striking number of ghazals in your work, especially in your first book *0°, 0°*. Was this early interest in the ghazal connected with your (occasional) channeling of middle-easternness? Or was there something about the form per se, apart from its cultural associations, that drew you to it?

AM: The greatest advantage to the ghazal was, and is, that the majority of its examples in English either fail to actually meet the criteria of the form, or are horrible poems, or both. That sure isn't the case with the sonnet. Also I knew ghazals firsthand from my knowledge of Ghalib in the original Urdu, so I felt I had an advantage. The ghazal is also the most unabashed of all forms— the most naked repetition and periodicity. It's a way of publicly owning up to artifice, something generally considered a no-no in contemporary poetry.

DB: One of my favorites among your ghazals is "By Accident," from *0°, 0°* (which Heather McHugh selected for the 2007 *Best American Poetry* volume). I'm especially struck by this provocative couplet: "Only surfaces interest me./ What depths I sound I sound by accident." Ashbery questions the very distinction between surface and depth (the surface being "not/ Superficial but a visible core"). But if, as I suspect, you'd question this questioning—if you'd say there *is* such a thing as depth as distinguishable from surface—is depth really something you're not interested in pursuing? (Most poets would go in fear of being called superficial, even—perhaps especially—by themselves.) Or maybe it's just that you don't think depth is *susceptible* of (intentional) pursuit? (Or maybe the "Amit" of "By Accident" isn't you at all but what Dickinson called a "supposed person," and the real Amit is at least open to sounding depths on purpose . . . ?)

AM: "The Sufi is the son of the moment," goes an old Persian saying. And so is the poet. That poem is almost a decade old, and I can scarcely remember, much less defend, what I wrote last month. I often make declarative verse statements more because they sound interesting than because they are literally true. *Right now,* in August of 2015, I consider surface and depth to occupy the same space and time as the poem itself. A black hole is bottomless precisely because it is so dense, so solid; its depth has been purified of emptiness. A solid poem should exist in much the same state—and sometimes, in select cases, serve as a wormhole into another universe.

DB: In your first collection, published when you were thirty, you'd already come well into your own. *0°, 0°* displays many of your distinguishing and defining characteristics: imagination, loose-limbed and associative thought, an ambitious range of subjects crossing many large domains of nature and culture, a pursuit (and conquest) of formal techniques . . . I'm wondering what your still earlier work—given your prolificacy, one suspects there was plenty—was like. Was it influenced by a particular poet or poets? Can you identify any milestones in your progression to poetic maturity?

AM: My *first* first book was self-published when I was seventeen. It was called *Entrance* and was a few hundred pages long. It was in three parts. The first consisted of philosophical quatrains that imitated Emily Dickinson. I even got one of my *Entrance* quatrains published in a magazine, years later—it was called "Picnic"—

> There is much casual in death,
> Much random at our last,
> As if God, chatting on a lawn,
> Were picking at the grass.

The second and third parts of *Entrance* consisted of narrative blank verse and blank verse dramas that imitated Shakespeare. The main verse drama was a five-act play about Don Juan and the Commendador [sic] of Stone. After *Entrance,* I became a nuclear radiologist, got married, had twins, and rewrote and re-erased my literary self several times until the mixed-up east-west palimpsest of everything I've ever read is finally who I am for now. For the record, though, the first things I ever wrote seriously were spy novels starring James Bond (I didn't understand copyright infringement at age twelve).

DB: And *my* first stab was a Tom Swift knockoff . . . But enough about me. Your poetry rarely *sounds* like Whitman—and then only slightly—but one might see a kindredship to his capaciousness in it. (One of your personas, *Dothead*'s Khwaja Mustasim, literally "contain[s] multitudes," as Whitman said of himself—and in fact Mustasim adduces Whitman when he pays a remarkable visit to your contributor's note for "his" poem in *The Best of the Best American Poetry*.) And of course Whitman had his own way—if very different from yours—of amalgamating East (via Emerson) and West . . . All of the above notwithstanding, I don't recall seeing any mention of Whitman (unless you count Mustasim's) in your poetry or prose. Was his work to any degree an inspiration? Do you even see a connection, or is this just a wrong tree to be barking up?

AM: First of all, let me assert that "Song of Myself" is a reworking of Books X and XI of the *Bhagavad-Gita*—the ones where Krishna describes, in first person, his Universal Form. The spirit of "Song of Myself" is closer to the *Gita* than to the voice of the whirlwind in the Book of Job. (If Whitman never knew the *Gita,* then the parallelism is literary proof of something mystics have never needed proof of.) Most American critics of Whitman haven't studied Eastern religions deeply enough to see the unity of the Sanskrit "Song of God" and the American "Song of Myself"; it's like the generations that used to read Virgil with no knowledge of Homer. Mystically considered, the titles of the two poems are identical, except for the substitution of a synonym. The unity of "God" and "My Self" is at the heart of all mystical doctrine, whether Upanishadic or Sufi or Emersonian-Transcendentalist.

I came to Whitman late, but he taught me a few things, not all of which I am willing to apply to my own practice. Foremost of which is that any amount of verbal slovenliness can be carried across by force of personality. Readers are more interested in a personality than in artistry. A poet *is* a literary character of sorts, the speaker of his or her poems, who "exists" in the same way a dramatist's or novelist's characters "exist." Emily, Famous Seamus, Pablo Neruda—they are people we visit with, getting to know and love them through their words the way we get to know and love characters in fiction and people in real life.

With Whitman, the poems are frequently just occasions to spend time with this voluble enthusiastic mystic American. The hollow, inflated nature of the majority of his individual lines is proof of his superior force of personality. The proportion of dross can be massive, he taught me, as long as there is some anthologizable gold in there somewhere, and above all the presence of a *personality* people like and can relate to.

Ashbery understands this best among recent poets. The poems can say any damned thing any damned how, as long as they successfully embody a friend. This is a bitter truth to stomach for the great polishers and line-filers of the world—the Wilburesque craftsmen of the art who never quite enrapture a culture. After the lines reach a certain degree of competence, everything floats or sinks on the basis of force of personality. No matter how tight its rigging, an oeuvre can still sink to the bottom of the sea.

DB: Would it be wrong to say that this learning from Whitman is reflected in the "bigness" of *Dothead?* Much material there, and some quite long poems—e.g. the prose poem "Abecedarian," a hymn to and about fellatio (largely) which is all the more astonishing for the length to which you vitally sustain it . . . And if you do see this sort of "size" as new to *Dothead,* are there any other characteristics you see as being so?

AM: The presiding spirit over *Dothead,* as over all of my works, is Goethe. Whitman strikes me as curiously all of a piece, circumscribed in his scope. His proclamations of multifariousness are not matched by a willingness or capacity to inhabit other ways of looking at the universe. He doesn't "speak" other religions and time periods like Goethe, the author of the "Mahomets Gesang" and the "Classical Walpurgisnacht." Goethe the writer was formally protean but intellectually integrated. The plethora of forms in *Dothead* have their precursor in *Faust* and Goethe's lyric output, not in the monotonies of *Leaves of Grass*. You noticed I write ghazals; Goethe wrote a whole *West-Easterly Diwan,* modeled after Hafiz. Goethe died in 1832, and after him, you see these outsized but fundamentally dis-integrated geniuses of the 19th century. Victor Hugo, at roughly the same time he drafted the secular populist novel *Les Miserables,* was also drafting *Dieu* and *La Fin de Satan,* massive religious epics in rhymed couplets. He was a divided mind, the political and secular on one side, the mystic and religious on the other. Tolstoy went through his famous psychological and stylistic break after *Anna Karenina,* coming out the other side a Christian anarchist writer of parables and polemics. Flaubert swung wildly from the hallucinatory visions of *La Tentation de Saint-Antoine* clear over to Madame Bovary's shopping-bills right back to the crucified lions of *Salammbô.* These men wanted to write the otherworldly and the worldly, but they couldn't manage to unify everything literarily.

Dostoyevsky did it in *The Brothers Karamazov,* perhaps, and Yeats in his later books—but I suppose by the 1930s it was necessary to integrate even more to possess a fully integrated mind. By which I mean capital-S Science. We cannot be totally modern poets anymore without incorporating, to some degree, the drastic surge in our scientific knowledge; yet Goethe was a scientist, too—a precursor of Darwin, in fact. Goethe's was the last global mind in the West. He is the presiding spirit over *Dothead,* and my full-on pursuit of the Goethean is what is new in *Dothead.*

DB: Bacon said "there is no excellent beauty but doth have some strangeness in the proportion." Your work seems to me replete with irruptions of a salutary and *echt-*poetic strangeness (exemplified, for instance, by the "sniff weevils" that creep up the inside of a roan's nostrils in *Dothead*'s "Horse Apocalypse"). Would you acknowledge this quality in your work? If so, do you share Bacon's sense of its value? And if you do, is it something you make a particular point of pursuing? (The avowed surrealist Dean Young makes no bones about being explicitly after the associative leaps in his poems.)

AM: I do agree with Bacon on that, but I would point out that a tremendous amount of bad poetry has been written in the conscious pursuit of strangeness for its own sake.

Dean Young's surrealism is not quite surrealism, to my eye; he is always aiming at the heart, at poignant or funny or quirky-poignant or quirky-funny. Surrealism originated in the visual arts, and it emphasized the novelty of the juxtapositions. Dean Young isn't content with this, and he doesn't make the imagery itself the focus (pun intended) of his poetry; that is, he does not set a mustached elephant on stilts for the mere effect of it. His associative leaps are usually the juxtaposition of unalike but self-contained, affectively charged images. He emphasizes the emotion or mood, not the visual weirdness. (In fact his technique is quite close to the ghazal, only he works at the level of the verse sentence instead of the couplet.)

As for me, I avoid pursuing strangeness on purpose; I may seem strange but it is quite "by accident." I attain poetic strangeness, if I attain it at all, by seeking the apt in strange places. When I wrote about those sniff weevils, I thought, "Okay, that's apt—that's exactly what a horse would think if it were in WWI and thought it were living through the apocalypse and went blind from mustard gas . . ."

DB: Most poets are content to make poems. You seem to want to make something more (and I don't just mean novels). "Now shall I make my soul," said Yeats. You seem to want to make, if not your soul, at least your mind—and to judge from your Goethian aspiration, your wish for that mind is that it be "global" (to the extent that that's still possible). Do you at all recognize yourself in these impressions? If so, how would you characterize the relation between your poetic aspirations and your personal ones? Might you see the forging of your mind as your fundamental pursuit, and your poetry as a by-product or artifact of it? Or perhaps you see the writing of poems as integral to—maybe even the heart of—that pursuit? (Emerson saw the writing of a poem as a "lever" that can elevate the poet to a higher plane of understanding.)

AM: "The *anima,* the animal, the man: the mind, the I, the eye:/ What is it that I forge before this I Am that I am must die?"

Even if I all cared to do was make verses on the side, like an Elizabethan man of the world, the making of verses would be no trivial thing because the making of beauty is no trivial thing. Poetry is the noble pursuit of a nobility: I say "nobility" because poets and readers of poetry are a hidden nobility, possessed of richness of language and the richest sensitivity to language, by birth and cultivation; I say "noble" because poetry is fundamentally unworldly, if not anti-worldly, even when it looks most closely at the world—for its gaze is piercing, and it looks *through* the world, as through a glass brightly.

I say "noble"—but poetry-making makes a terrible Emersonian "lever" to raise a mind to self-understanding, as the vanity of poets shows. May I own up to vanity and self-delighting virtuosity as the earliest engines of my creativity? The wish to be famous, the wish to be loved and well-spoken of by strangers. This was true especially when I was a teenager. And then, in my twenties, I conceived the ambition to make the Upanishads and the *Ramayana* as indispensable to understanding American literature as the Bible and the Fall are to understanding English literature; to stand in relation to all Hindu poets as Dante stands in relation to all Christian ones. Now, in my thirties, the wish to be a total, Goethean human being—how silly, how downright psychiatric these things sound when written down in rational prose!

And yet: *Psyche,* soul. Naturally all these daydreams go unfulfilled, because they are quite impossible. But that is the point, isn't it? That is the bait-and-switch in which the Gods and the Muses conspire. I can see myself, over the past few decades, trying to create a better poet, and, in the quest for a better rhyme, creating a better human being. (I hope?) Poetry has given my life discipline, too, as weirdly severe as any monastic rule. The chimerical, shifting vanishing-points of worldly and literary ambition have tricked me into self-improvement. Rhyme is a schemer; rhyme scams us into truth. But this itself is a poet's vanity, this claim I have bettered myself, spiritually and intellectually, by my involvement with this art. I am probably more self-absorbed and finicky about time management than a father of three little kids should be. I mean, I *did* just spend a few thousand words talking about myself . . .

DB: For what my opinion is worth, I think your ambition *is* noble, and I admire you for it. And you surely have some good company in your wish to do great things (the teenaged Frost spoke, in a striking phrase, of "the astonishing magnitude of my ambition," even if that ambition had dwindled in later life—if this is dwindling—to a desire to "lodge a few poems where they'll be hard to get rid of"). I'd also imagine that great aims suggest themselves most readily and compellingly to those who can achieve them (or, if those aims are "chimerical," at least pursue them fruitfully) . . . Joyce famously posited a natural progression for a literary career from lyric to narrative to epic. Your "big-picture" sense of your own development makes we wonder if you have any such vision for its future?

AM: I do, but the details shift by the moment. Joyce's notion is based in a very old hierarchy in Western literature, where the epic poets are always considered the top dogs. Epic > Tragic Drama > Short Poetry, goes the traditional thinking, and the pressure of that is why lyric masters like Petrarch insisted on writing the *Africa* and Tennyson insisted on writing the *Idylls of the King.*

The hierarchy still holds; we see it, in the contemporary West, in the preferential treatment given (by everyone—publishers, the media, and readers) to novelists, to the Great American Novel. Yet in the classical traditions of the Far East, you find that their most revered writers—Basho, Tu Fu, Li Po—wrote very small poems; in Persia, the greatest poets are writers of ghazals and ruba'i like Rumi and Hafiz, while long-form narrative poets like Firdausi and Nizami are less read, less revered, and less loved.

I want to find a power and perfection distinct to me with no regard to these culturally determined hierarchies: whether in the form of verse or prose, short lyric or poem infinite, or essay or novel or screenpoem, or translation or memoir or criticism, I do not know. Everything I attempt begins with the same hope—that this will be it, this will be powerful and perfect and true. It never is. So I begin again.

Featured Poetry
New Poems from Amit Majmudar
★ ★ ★

Amit Majmudar

No Future

Novas happen when God wants eggs for breakfast.
Stands to reason he'd reason he could break us.

Love me, said our Maker. We the mad
Said *Come over here and make us.*

Old rivers, new dams. Old farms,
New lakes. Their stillness shakes us.

Descended from the apes and
Descending like the locusts

We follow our drive to possess
Until we get where it takes us.

We made God make the cosmos in our
Image: Mons Venus, solar plexus.

We will make what we have always made
Until the things we make unmake us.

Amit Majmudar

Excerpt from an Intelligence Hearing

"... Their ideas were not unbeautiful.
The moles among us were gentlemen, aesthetes,
really, drawn by a love of symmetry
to photographs of workers on parade.
Drawn, too, by the love of a tale well told
to Marx's world-historical ever-after
in a wheat field enthroned on a tractor,
that future past-like, charmingly pastoral . . .
Of course we both believed in equality,
and this striving to outequal one another
rendered inevitable our rivalry.
Their ideas, I say, were not unbeautiful;
we argued them at University
and championed, in our loafers, the downtrodden
workers of the world. We saw their reasons,
saw their essential nobility of purpose
before we entered the Service and swore
an oath to destroy them. We were young men,
and not fanatical; aesthetes, really,
drawn by a love of chiaroscuro
to years of shadow boxing in East Berlin,
drawn by a love of language, of poetry,
to decrypt those signal intercepts
that whispered of dark and distant submarines
bearing their burdens miles beneath the sea."

Amit Majmudar

Chronic Pain

You know one by that right hook to the chin
look of a boxer bleeding on the ropes,
that trapped and thinking two-foot mammal in
a basement cage look. Not the loss of hope;

hope defined unrecognizably down
to half a day with pain at six out of ten
thanks to a needlestick and Vicodin
and appointments on opposite sides of town.

The body can become a torture camp,
its spinal cord a juiced electric cable
hooked to your brain with an alligator clamp

while up there, on the waiting room TV,
talk-show ladies complain around a table
and Carnival cruise lines promise you the sea.

Amit Majmudar

Protest Poem

Where are the radicals of yesteryear
with their vans and sandalwood and Dylan songs?
I don't mean the ones who have tenure here:

I mean the prophets with pollen-peppered beards,
grand plans and sandy hair and trombone bongs.
Where are the radicals of yesteryear,

the ones the shields and nightsticks used to fear?
Where are the girls with acid on their tongues
who'd rather die than chair a department here?

Where are the tear gas breathers, foolish-fierce?
Weren't they once a hundred thousand strong?
Where are the radicals of yesteryear,

the painters, panthers, chaos engineers
who called out might when might was wrong?
I've heard the radicals who lecture here—

they're not the same as those who disappeared
with their rants and sandal tans and singalongs.
Where are the radicals of yesteryear?
Are we supposed to be the rebels here?

Amit Majmudar

The Strike-Anywhere Match

Strike anywhere, the sky, your ribs, the floor,
        and this euphoric phosphate head will flare
                in *Cosmos sulfureus,* furious flower

you can pluck from the surface of things, like New World cod
        so packed in the bay, a settler walked across
                their solid breeding waters deck to dock.

I slip one from a book and wave it like
        a magic wand, a pen, a lightning strike
                signing away a woodland with a stroke.

Who knew that so much fire hid in things,
        that, stricken anywhere, their smart and sting
                could spark awake to let the spirit sing?

My father taught my mouth to speak the truth
        when he slashed my cocky smile with one of these
                and struck a tongue of fire from my teeth.

Joachim du Bellay

Roman Holiday

Tourist, you've sought Rome
In what is not Rome:

These arches, villas, vias
Are how Rome, having fought Rome,

Vanquished, vanished,
Unwrought Rome.

The Rome of the laws is a lost Rome,
A word, unwhispered, a thought-Rome

Rivering past the Tiber.
What its waters taught Rome:

Time that thinks Rome,
Inks Rome, will blot Rome,

While Rome, by changing form,
Will stay, forever, not Rome.

— *Translated from the French[2] of Joachim du Bellay
by Amit Majmudar*

---

[2] See "Translation Notes" on page 121 for the original French version

FICTION

Lynda Sexson
Why Were You Sighing?

A snapshot loosens from oblivion, floating into the present and onto the carpet. Long ago, when it had been unworthy to fit into an album's little black mounting corners, the photo was tossed like Cupid on a Bicycle into a stack of paper.

Maybe third cousins. Or old next-door neighbors. Not from the Irish clan or the Italian hillbillies, they must be the Norwegians. Two *heftig* women stand with a *tynn* young man between them. A still life of two rutabagas flanking a carrot. Two radishes and a scallion. Two crosspatches and a rapscallion.

The women forget to tuck one heel against the other instep, the pastor's wife's recipe for a flattering look. Their platform sandals point like hands on a clock at ten to two; from the camera's view, twenty to five. Inside a photograph the hands of a clock refuse to tell time, but the picture always gives away instant and era. The shutter opens and closes on a moment in mid-twentieth century.

Maybe they never saw the picture, which remained undeveloped in the camera until another subject came up worthy of the last two shots left on the roll.

Memento Mori

They are saying I didn't go in for the noisy pleasures. They hunted around and only came up with this snapshot. I didn't even have wedding pictures made; thought to wait until I wasn't showing and then it seemed beside the point. Oh, yah, I didn't want to be in a photograph that day. Now it's the last sight of me. They are saying I made the coffee strong. *Bønner er bønner*. Prayers are beans.

The women cross their arms under their bosoms, their hands tucked away out of sight, tension in their forearms.

The boy has put his arms around the women, his hands spreading over their shoulders. Fingers like feathers. A great bird with two angry frogs.

> *History*
>
> The one on the boy's left had worked in a candy factory where the women took up smoking because of worms in the candy. The boy's outfit reminds her of the white jacket and hairnet she wore while plucking little visible white worms off the candies.
>
> The one on the boy's right will fall sick. A young man, almost like this young man, all in white, will come to her room. He will tell her that her breast has been removed. Her glasses are missing. The boy in the doctor's coat will resemble the dear boy who used to win every time at Crazy Eights, who once stood with them in the sunlight.

Smiles straight as rulers. The stretched skin of the women's smiles leaves no leftover flesh for upturns. They forget to say cheese. The boy says cheese. Their noses sundial late-afternoon, bulbous shadows across their lips.

The young man in the photo is scrawnier than a Norski. But he is handsome, with generous, big eyes. If he's related to these women, the Italians had been at the Norwegians. Maybe the Irish.

A goose urges two hens toward the sky. An angel teaches two souls to levitate. The souls stumble, chucking their image like a photograph into the angle of today.

> *Apocalypse*
>
> For an Angel appeared, coming with the clouds through the firmament of sapphire. He walked up and down upon the earth, his sandals leveling the mountains. And his wings gathered to him scattered souls like chickens.
>
> The angel sounded as a trumpet, *why were you sighing?* And the angel asked them, what do you see?
>
> The souls turned and answered, we see sunflowers higher than angels.
>
> And the angel asked again, what do you see?
>
> The souls turned and answered, stones are as a wheel round about the flowers. The flowers are as wheels within the wheel of stones.
>
> And the angel called out again, *why were you sighing?*

Sisters. Or mother and daughter. They shyly, bravely, wait for the camera to shoot them. The boy gives them the tenderness they might offer him.

Psychoanalysis

... *the course taken by mental events is regulated by the pleasure principle.* Mama had given her Eskimo kisses and butterfly kisses and bird kisses. Then she stopped.

Mama had taught her a verse about a *hyrden og feen:* a shepherd and a fairy. The girl learned to recite nonsense words, never learning what the verse meant, except that the poor shepherd's *arm var av.* Mama never went on with the lesson of how to count past *en, to, tre,* or how a shepherd might be *hakket opp* by a fairy. Years later the girl could not name what she feared or what she desired.

One dress from J.C. Penney's. The blue one from the Sears and Roebuck catalog. The boy is dressed in white for work. White shoes. A thin black belt.

An uncanny duplicate of the picture shows up on Facebook, defying photography's claim to capture an unrepeatable moment. Foreshadowed by monkeys at typewriters, Facebook digitizes time's unique events into patterns of infinity, like seeds on sunflowers.

Another slender young man is also a head taller than another pair of plump women. He also clasps their shoulders with fingers like feathers.

Facebook

Just a post to our friends that we are now married in the sight of the law, legal in both the state where we live and the state where Mom lives. Coast to coast. This is our nephew. We used to make Lego castles with him. Now so tall. We are still grading papers, logging birds, defending wetlands, and now married. From sea to shining sea.

Though the Facebook image commemorates love, erotic as well as filial, the nearly identical old snapshot does not, in any daft combination, configure lovers. But the night before, the women in the snapshot had put up each other's hair in pin curls, dividing the rows with a rat-tail comb, setting each curl with sugar water for a coiffure stylish since the Venus of Willendorf.

The boy and the women take up the lower half of the snapshot that rises into a Kodachrome sky.

Romance

Fresh from the sea and into the room came the handsomest man on water or land. The girl would say, I loved his scrinchy little Norwegian eyes.

He saw her eyes before he noticed she was knocked up. He asked her to marry him.

The mama and the auntie were glad enough he was done with the lady who dyed her hair and had hit him over the head with a frying pan. This one, loyal as a Collie dog, would never dye her hair.

> They were glad he was off the tugs to work his dad's dairy. He put the girl in the little house up the road and gave her money for curtains.
> The mama and the auntie worried what they would call a stranger's baby.
> The stork dropped his bundle and they called the baby their darling dumpling dandy big boy. They gave their baby Eskimo kisses and butterfly kisses and bird kisses.
> One day the mama, thinking of the baby, asked, how is *elskling;* the handsomest man at sea or on land, thinking of his new wife, said he liked her wide-bottomed yellow skirt. One turned rosy, the other turned pale.

Sunflowers, within an encircling border of stones, stand behind the three figures in the photo. Sunflowers stand twice as tall as humans, with bigger, blooming heads. As sunflowers go, these won't be going to the fair. They're roadside flowers, not a roadside attraction. Nothing in the picture is for the record book or an album. But the flowers put forth the impressive surge of a single season, offering whole platters of birdseed in Fibonacci spirals.

Fable

> Once the river dried up and stranded two turtles on a stone. A heron came and knocked on their shells with his long, thin beak. Why don't you move to the mountain lake of shimmering blue water? The turtles said they didn't know the way; they'd just make do. They crossed their arms inside their shells. I will take you, offered the heron. The turtles knew about the appetites of herons. I cannot eat you; your shells are much too hard, he said, tapping on them again. He put them in his basket and soared toward the sun. Too high, too swift, too far, they cried. In another story, in another time, the heron would overturn the basket, tumbling them onto the rocks, cracking them open and feasting. But in this picture the heron embraces the turtles as birds of a feather. When they reached the shining mountain lake the heron set them out to bask upon a log. The turtles pulled in their heads asking, when will you take us back to our stone?

In the old photograph a young man enfolds two women as summer dries up behind them. The heads of the sunflowers spiral both left and right.

Athar C. Pavis

Ode to Silence

    for H.

Here's to the silence of unspoken word,
The heart held in abeyance, like a clam,
Shut tight against indifference, but still heard
By men who give these nameless things a name—

Who never watch reality TV,
Nor rush to reconnect at Wi-Fi stations,
Who apprehend implicits, and that we
Lose them, in our *relationship discussions*.

Here's to the wordless hurts that do not whine,
Begging for recognition, and remain
Silent, as pulp psychologists opine
Better for mental health that they complain.

Here's to the silence before SMS,
Instant translator of our ups and downs,
Became the inner life we could express
Cheaply; before emoticons, like clowns

Pulled a long face, exaggerated smile,
To summarize the soul. This age of noise,
"You should have had the balls to speak," this style
Everyone shares, this feelingness that cloys,

Like squeezing a banana in your fist—
This is the Age of Treacle, someone said,
And Facebook gripes. How has self come to this—
As if these tell-all postings, half-unread,

Were proof of being? Let silence reign
In the unspeakable chasm they perceive,
Mothers whose only gift from life is pain,
Prodigal sons, lovers who cannot grieve—

Here's to the gated silence in the pause
Poets can hear, while glib men only post,
What Beckett found in wordlessness, because
Saying nothing sometimes says the most.

Catharine Savage Brosman

The Pianist and the Cicada

Aix-en-Provence, 1962

The cloistered court of the archbishopric
is full. It's summer. The piano's there.
There's stirring, expectation; dusk is thick
with garden sounds. Then Rubinstein, his flair

upon his sleeve, arrives. First, Chopin, Brahms,
both very brief. He wipes his beading face.
More Chopin. A cicada in the palms
begins to sing—a southern commonplace.

The master shapes the phrases: tender—tense—
expressive. Through the notes, however, comes
the insect's steady song. The audience
grows nervous, hearing their duet: one hums

insistently; the other strokes the keys,
hot-tempered, though. He could ignore a cough
or shuffling feet; not mating calls from trees.
He was about to start Rachmaninoff.

He pauses; the cicada pauses, too,
but sings again when he begins to play.
The prelude falls apart—a Waterloo.
He rises, bangs the lid, and strides away.

There is no refund; nature does not care,
nor management, it seems, nor Rubinstein,
the least of all. We can't be unaware
we're often nothing in the grand design.

Steven Winn

The Purpose of This Object Is Not Certain

Museum wall label

Forty golden Buddhas sit, recline, or stand
in five neat rows with forms aligned,
painted that way by some nameless
artist on this scoop-shaped slab of teak
for reasons now, to us, unknown.

Each Buddha gets a lotus filigree,
with blossom pillows for the seated ones
and everywhere the flare of leafy branches,
the writhing frozen fire of belief,
the sublimity of simply being there.

The pattern here might be the floors
of some cutaway-view department store,
the whole contraption held aloft by a giant
demon down below, shoulders bowed to hoist
the weight he balances on one furled toe.

It must be bliss to be a Buddha, eyes painted
shut and not (exactly) existing up there
on the wall, on a wooden form that we're
left wondering what it's for. Imagine snow:
Then this thing could be the first Thai sled.

Purposes are often puzzling matters—
but isn't that what meditation's after,
to know it finally doesn't matter
if that's grin or grimace on the demon's face,
and if he's barely bearing up—or dancing.

Jay Udall

Tools of the Trade

It was tough killing each other with stones.
I mean, if you could catch a guy sleeping
you'd just drop a big one on his head, but
more often he'd spot you lugging that thing
his way, and run. Then someone realized
a spear was good for more than hunting, though
issues with distance and running remained
until addressed by the speed and piercing
precision of an arrow's tip let go
from a string of hide stretched tight—such quiet
dread whole armies rained on each other's heads.
Yet I confess nostalgia for the knife,
a hand-spear with facets of surprise and
intimacy. You had to look a guy
in the eyes or, if you chose to backstab,
firmly clasp his shoulder with your free hand
in an almost brotherly way as you
slipped the blade in—shades of Abel and Cain,
family business, a living tradition.
Guns? Invented by cowards. Any fool
can kill, and the poor victim might as well
be an *idea,* for God's sake, a distant
abstraction, even more so when you drop
a bomb from the sky like some kind of god,
even worse when you press a button to
launch missile or drone, turn away to play
eighteen holes. Where's the sport in that, the warmth
and humanity, so far and so clean—
where is the murderer in the machine?

Beth Houston

Ice

As traffic hushes, rain slows, chilled dusk stills.
Fogged windows darken, thinning chimney smoke
Drifts up and hovers, frosted streetlight spills
On hardened puddles; wrapped in silken cloak,
Ice slips black gloves from slick black hands, they peel
The moon to make sleep potions of eclipse
And spells that freeze park fountains, hands that steal
The verve and verdant stunned by smooth cold lips
That sip the rain, that tease each pose to change
Into a poise devoid of change, that trick
Each drip to slowly cease to drip: this strange
New liquid, icicle, extends with slick
    Fresh form first form, each solid water slice
    Of light more crystal once it melts to ice.

Beth Houston

The Ghost Nudges Me to the Cellar

I swore I would have oiled the squeaky door
And nailed these creaking stairs, swept clear the floor,
Replaced the rusted socket with a light
That never flickers, all before this chore.

If my ghost watching me suspected fright
One gleans from gothic novels, she'd be right.
Cool, musty drafts push spider webs, and poor
Spooked mice go skittering in futile flight.

I've two large buckets full of bulbs, and more
Upstairs and in the ground, but these I pour
Out gently on the workbench, more polite
Than one might tolerate an old aunt's snore.

Exotic bulbs so tender that they might
Not make it through the first hard freeze tonight.
At first I thought I might as well ignore
The warnings of the catalogs in spite

Of every urge in me to dig and store.
But though this stiff bent back can't take much more
With all this stooping, I expect delight
Next spring and summer, like I have before.

You taunt my laziness, my failing sight.
But I'm the type that puts up quite a fight
For underlings. So now you know the score,
Just leave me be, ghost. Mice scratch for a bite,

I hear them in the walls and ceiling, drawer
And tool chest, nooks where I had planned to store
These flowers holding moist and seasoned light
Coiled up inside their trusting fleshy core.

I brush the dirt off—careful, simple rite—
In one hand hold the whole year's cycle tight:
My hand's more layered chaff. Fall's precious ore
Grasps living's chemistry that can excite

An old crone to recall her hands, her sore,
Red, calloused touch still eager to explore
Dug magical spring flowers taking flight—
I hear their breathing, dreaming, quiet roar.

BOOK REVIEW

Robert B. Shaw

A Review of Catherine Breese Davis,
On the Life and Work of an American Master
Edited by Martha Collins, Kevin Prufer, & Martin Rock,
The Unsung Masters Series, Pleiades Press, 2015
ISBN 978-0-9641454-6-7, 224 pp., USA $12.99, paperback

★ ★ ★

When poetry of unusual merit, held back in obscurity for many years, finally reaches the public, appreciative readers naturally are pleased that justice has been done. That certainly is one feeling prompted by this long-awaited selection of the work of Catherine Davis (1924-2002). Posthumous justice, though, always carries a bittersweet tang, and this volume invites an array of complex reactions. One feels disgusted at a literary culture that could find no place for Davis's talents during her lifetime, as well as dismay at numerous bad personal and professional choices of hers that helped to keep her poems in limbo. And after reading and rereading her work it is hard to say what feeling dominates: admiration for a remarkable gift for verse technique, bemusement at a sensibility that seems so deeply alien to mid-twentieth-century America, or simple alarm at what many of her poems have to say. Her most memorable writing is deeply subversive of our society's complacencies.

Davis was born into bad luck, and seems to have escaped it only sporadically and for brief intervals. This volume is valuable for providing in its secondary materials far more information than has been available before about the dismal facts of her life. Can a less favorable background for any poet be imagined? Davis's father was sent to prison for armed robbery when she was an infant; upon his release he did not return to the family. Her mother farmed out Catherine and her sister to foster homes and relatives while pursuing relationships with a number of men, one of whom owned a bar and for whom she managed his second business, a brothel. When Catherine's mother discovered that her daughter was a lesbian, she drove the future poet, then sixteen, to a train station and left her there, never seeing or speaking to her again.

Moreover, Davis had some major physical and behavioral problems to struggle with. She was born with a mild form of cerebral palsy, misdiagnosed as polio while she was growing up, which affected her left side in function and mobility. She was, for much of her adult life, an alcoholic. These and many more personal details are aired in a remarkable interview the editors conducted with Marie Pelletier, Davis's companion for several years. Marie Pelletier, additionally, suggests that Davis was what would now be termed bipolar. This seems not to have been medically attested, but it certainly fits her friends' descriptions of her mood swings and her tendency to make life hard for herself and others.

There are not too many bright spots in this story. One of the few is Davis's good fortune in finding a series of mentors and poet friends who generously fostered her development during her often interrupted, drawn-out education. (She attended a number of colleges, finally receiving her BA at thirty-seven.) The teaching and encouragement of J.V. Cunningham, Yvor Winters, and Allen Tate was crucial to her writing early on; somewhat later, when she pursued a Master's degree at the Iowa Workshop, she forged a bond of friendship with Donald Justice, who made serious attempts to have a book of her poems published. Friends from the Winters circle at Stanford and others from her time at Iowa attempted over the years to promote her work, and at times it must have seemed that her career was poised to take off. Poems would appear in well-regarded magazines and anthologies, but a volume never materialized.

Davis brought out three slender pamphlet collections for which she set the type herself and which had limited circulation. In the meantime she bounced from one short-term academic job to another, with less appealing kinds of employment in between—for example, selling tickets at a movie theater in Boston's Combat Zone. The kind of traditional verse that was her forte went out of fashion in the Sixties and Seventies, and Davis, discouraged by her failure to find a publisher and no doubt depleted by the hardships of living on or, eventually, over the brink of poverty, gave up writing for a number of years. She made a last stab at assembling a book-length selection of poems in 1995, but this too found no takers. To the ever-narrowing circle of friends with whom she stayed in touch, her career and indeed her life must have seemed something like a slow-motion train wreck.

Davis died destitute in a nursing home, to which she had been moved when Alzheimer's made it impossible for her to live alone. She died intestate and without any record of living relatives. These circumstances have continued until now to keep her work out of print, since publishers have been unwilling to risk a dispute over rights, if an heir were to surface. Some years ago Helen Pinkerton Trimpi (who knew Davis at Stanford) and

Suzanne Doyle compiled a selection of her poems which they were unable to bring out because of the lingering legal shadow. There things remained stalled until the present editors succeeded in locating Davis's nephew, who was happy to give permission for her poems to be published. And here they are.

This book differs in its contents and format from the selection attempted by Trimpi and Doyle. In keeping with the practice of the Unsung Masters Series, it includes not only Davis's poems but commentaries by a number of hands and some secondary materials by Davis herself. And, we are told, it attempts to represent the phases and facets of Davis's writing more inclusively than did Trimpi and Doyle, who gave more space to Davis's writing in traditional verse forms and less to her later experiments in free verse.

That there *were* such experiments will come as news to many who have viewed Davis, if they have heard of her at all, as a formalist in the mold of Cunningham and Winters. Certainly her earlier poems are some of the most notable modern examples of the plain style that Winters traced back to Renaissance models such as Raleigh, Jonson, and Greville, emulated himself, and encouraged in his students. Davis's eventual deviations from the mode deserve comment, but it is important to acknowledge first the preeminence of her formalist pieces. Curiously, her most traditional verses seem her most original. She writes with meditative depth as a lyricist, and with trenchant force as a satirist. Winters anthologized several of her epigrams, which she grouped under the heading "Insights." It would be hard to outdo the corrosive pithiness of her view of literary society, "In New York," which begins, "What can I do here? I could learn to lie;/ Mouth Freud and Zen," and ends, "New York is something new:/ The toadies like the toads they toady to." Her epigrams recall Cunningham's, but just as insistently Renaissance and Classical models: Jonson and Herrick, Martial and Catullus. And like theirs, hers carry a moral weight that makes them more than diverting trinkets. It is riveting when she makes herself the target of her unsparing satirist's eye, as in "Insight 7: Imitation of Some Lines by Catullus":

> Idleness, wretch, idleness ruins you!
> Idleness works by more than mere inaction:
> Exalts, among the great, great idlers, too,
> And plunges you in riot and distraction.

Davis's meditative lyrics have the same searching penetration as her epigrams, while extending their arguments over greater length and in more intricate forms. Of her many fine poems, some of these are, I think, the most memorable of all. I would point especially to "What Does It Mean?," "Obsession," "After a Time," "Under This Lintel," "The Narrow House," and "The First Step." Others are almost as well wrought and almost as emotionally powerful. But these display the plain style as a diamond-bladed instrument, laying bare, as few modern poets have done, the human susceptibility to both self-wounding negation and self-deluding illusion. Her manner in such dark pieces is distinctly different from the emotional extremity of Confessional poets like Plath and Sexton. She shares nothing of their melodrama, nor of their gossipy circumstantial detail. She enters the material instead from a high level of abstraction. Although modern poetry has overwhelmingly championed the specific over the general, Davis demonstrates that divulging lurid particulars is not the only way to claim a reader's attention. She does it, it seems, through sheer conviction, the absolute control of tone, the unwavering directness of her style. Her voice is at times oracular, propounding not so much personal confidences as adages whose application is piercingly universal. When Sexton writes strongly, one thinks of Robert Lowell. When Davis is at the top of her form, one thinks of Job or Ecclesiastes. Not that there is anything biblically grand about her style: it is conversational, unadorned, eerie in its lucidity. Her poems are rarely hard to understand, and critics are challenged not so much to unpack her arguments as to assess the sense of radical aloneness—the insight, to use her word—that inspired them.

In Davis's internal colloquies, it is as if a door clicks shut in every stanza, leaving the soul no escape routes. Or perhaps only one. Her poem on the mental torments that spawn insomnia traces the chains that keep the speaker's restless present fettered to the past:

> I doze a little, dream, and start:
> The random terrors of the heart
> Wake me—they take my daemon's part:
>   What does it mean?

The increasingly hopeless weariness reaches its chilling climax in the eighth and final stanza:

> What does it matter that the past
> And my own daemon hold me fast?
> I shall get sleep enough at last.
>   What does it mean?

Of course, the reference here is to an ultimate kind of sleep, and even her resignation to that cannot silence the frustrated bafflement of the unrhymed refrain. The poem by Thomas Wyatt on which Davis's is modeled (with its refrain "What menys this?") is a lover's complaint; for Davis the source of suffering is not so easily assigned to erotic frustration, instead suggesting various forms of early trauma still haunting the adult speaker. Another refrain poem, "The Narrow House," is an equally harrowing treatment of the struggle to escape or to accept the phantoms of the past—both strategies fraught with pain:

> Who, looking back, can bear escape?
> Their presences, still grieving, gape;
> Who shuns their anguish takes their shape
>   In a narrow house.

Davis is one of the more impressive twentieth-century religious poets, if that category includes, as I think it must, exponents of doubt and spiritual dispossession. She was hardly singular for her time in deciding that the Christian promise of redemption was not for her. What makes her unusual is the cool, exacting argumentation of her apostasy, and her refusal to congratulate herself for it. "The First Step" brilliantly and perversely inverts St. Bernard's trope of the stair of humility. The speaker finds herself at a daunting turning point: "The downward flight, reversed,/ As I look back in dread,/ Ascends and disappears/ In shadow overhead." Bernard counseled his monks to go lower, step by step, to achieve humility; Davis, to whom "The last step is the first," finds there "Not God, nothing but pride." And she arraigns both a promise of Grace that seems beyond her reach and her own pride that maintains the unbridgeable gap:

> I see both whence I came
> And where I am, how far
> I've drifted who preferred
> My own fool vagrancy:
> If knowing this, I go
> My own way all the same,
> How does it help to know?

Perhaps even more immediately powerful, since it does not rely on theological reference, is the extraordinary villanelle, "After a Time," which was to have been the title poem of Trimpi and Doyle's projected selection. A hauntingly austere piece, it serves as a rebuke to the bluster of Dylan Thomas's villanelle, "Do Not Go Gentle into That Good Night," and must, as I have argued elsewhere, have given impetus to Elizabeth Bishop's later venture in the form, "One Art." Davis begins, "After a time, all losses are the same./ One more thing lost is one thing less to lose;/ And we go stripped at last the way we came." This is Davis at her most sibylline; the level, dispassionate tone seems to be not that of a twentieth-century poet, but of the human condition itself, whispering its unwelcome inside information deep in the reader's mind. For ordinary readers, Davis's most basic insight is also her most disturbing: that no one, ultimately, is exempt. Neither poets nor readers can sustain such a pitch; these stronger poems by Davis are best sampled in small doses. Helen Pinkerton Trimpi has contributed to this volume an acute essay on Davis's style and concerns in pieces treating what Trimpi identifies as her "theme of loss." Unquestionably, such poems stand at the center of her achievement, but they do not represent its sum. As previously mentioned, this selection shows how, in her Iowa years and later, Davis varied her verse forms, expanded her subject matter, and modulated her voice.

In a short prose statement, "The Air We Breathed," Davis herself speaks of the effect on her and other poets her age of the shaking up of style (as of much else) in the 1960s, and of the influence of Lowell's *Life Studies* and Williams's *Pictures from Brueghel*. At Iowa, she says, "I began to write, much to my own surprise, free verse while continuing to write formal poetry; others changed to free verse for good. . . . But I could never see why I should not practice both, as so many poets had done in the early twentieth century. Neither one is superior to the other." Davis's more experimental pieces are often highly accomplished, but their effect is more diffuse, lacking the icy concentration of her taut earlier stanzas. They offer a more personally revealing view of the poet's experience, as in the punishing free-verse portrait of her mother, "She," the gritty street scene, "Begging for Change," and the dejected love-as-disaster lyric, "To an Archeologist Some Years Hence." An ambitious sequence, "The Summer That Never Was," juxtaposes the assassinations of Martin Luther King and Robert Kennedy with Davis's own stay in a mental hospital. The sequence does not quite gel, but it is fascinating to see her own version of Lowell's conflations of personal and societal breakdowns in the Sixties. The most striking thing about the later work, more important than its prosodic shifts, is that it embraces scenic description, including sensory imagery far more than her previous work did. Scenes and objects become more particularized, differing from her earlier practice, in which metaphors are often so traditional as to seem archetypal, fielding vehicles such as light or shadow, the leaves that flourish or the leaves that fall. Now, when she reverts to formal versification, she applies it to a clear-eyed view of the world around her rather than exclusively probing her own inner dilemmas. One beautiful later poem, "A Small River in Iowa and the Wide World," conducts its argument as much through imagery as through self-analysis, as the first stanza shows:

> July, late afternoon. I sit alone
> And look at only water; the still river,
> On which the homely bridge's arches cast
> Three perfect oval mirrors less than a stone
> May break and break the stillness, soon will shiver
> With life, be lost, imperfect as the past.

Here the investing of nature with symbolic import is effectively done, and with a lighter touch.

As she moved beyond her early, sometimes claustrophobic introspection, Davis began to make room for glimpses of other people, some intimate, some fleeting. Her sonnet sequence, *"for tender stalkes,"* convincingly brings the form into the late twentieth century, chronicling its romantic misalliance with the same deftness she had brought to spiritual issues. And it is moving to find this conclusion, in what may be the last poem she completed, "Finding Ourselves and Others," written after a silence of seventeen years:

> But how hard
>   it is
>
> To be open, bear
> The differences of
> Others, or try to.
> If we can, a rare
> And radiant love,
> Now and then, breaks through.

Here, if one thinks back to the wrenching earlier poem "I Need More Light," the word "radiant," even if hedged with the cautious "Now and then," is especially touching.

This book wholly succeeds in its aim, to bring to the life and work of a virtually unknown poet some belated due attention. I hope that attention will focus chiefly on Davis's masterly verse rather than her ill-starred life. Her poems offer pleasures that are strikingly individualized, sometimes intense, and never cozy. The only complaint I have about this volume is that in it one of Davis's finer epigrams, "To the Spirit of Baudelaire," is marred by a typo. In the second line, what this text gives as "manic bird" must surely, as in Winters's anthology printing, be "mantic bird." Thus:

> *Wind of the wing of madness!* What is this?
> O you that shuddered then, what mantic bird?
> What travesty, dark spirit, of the Word?
> What last cold exhalation of your bliss?
> What passage to what end? Speechless abyss.

In her life, Davis, like Baudelaire, may have passed through manic phases; but the message both poets had for the world in their poetry was a mantic one—that is, one empowered with divination, delivered from the brink of the abyss.

AbleMUSE
A REVIEW OF POETRY, PROSE & ART

After more than a decade of online publishing excellence, Able Muse began a bold new chapter with its Print Edition

We continue to bring you in print the usual masterful craft with poetry, fiction, essays, art & photography, and book reviews

Check out our 12+ years of online archives for work by

RACHEL HADAS • X.J. KENNEDY • TIMOTHY STEELE • MARK JARMAN • A.E. STALLINGS • DICK DAVIS • A.M. JUSTER • TIMOTHY MURPHY • DEBORAH WARREN • CHELSEA RATHBURN • RHINA P. ESPAILLAT • TURNER CASSITY • RICHARD MOORE • STEPHEN EDGAR • ANNIE FINCH • THAISA FRANK • NINA SCHUYLER • SOLITAIRE MILES • MISHA GORDIN • & SEVERAL OTHERS

SUBSCRIPTION

Able Muse – Print Edition – Subscriptions:

Able Muse is published semiannually.
Subscription rates—for individuals: $24.00 per year; single and previous issues: $16.95 + $3 S&H.
International subscription rates: $33 per year; single and previous issues: $16.95 + $5 S&H.
(All rates in USD.)

Subscribe online with WePay/credit card **www.ablemusepress.com**

Or send a check payable to *Able Muse Review*
Attn: Alex Pepple – Editor, *Able Muse*, 467 Saratoga Avenue #602, San Jose, CA 95129 USA

Walking in on People
Poems
by Melissa Balmain

*NEW~ *from* Able Muse Press

WINNER
2013 Able Muse Book Award

PRAISE FOR *WALKING IN ON PEOPLE*
(with an foreword by David Yezzi)

The first full-length collection from Melissa Balmain

★★★★★

"Melissa Balmain's poems add to the rhythmic bounce of light verse a darker, more cutting humor."
— Billy Collins

"*Walking in on People* grabbed me with its very title, and it never let go . . . [Melissa Balmain] really commands her art."
— X.J. Kennedy
(Judge, 2013 Able Muse Book Award)

"So many of the poems in Melissa Balmain's triumphant debut lodge themselves in that Frostian zone where they are hard to get rid of."
— David Yezzi *(from the foreword)*

ISBN 978-1-927409-29-9 / 102 pages

ORDER NOW FROM ABLE MUSE PRESS AT: WWW.ABLEMUSEPRESS.COM
OR, ORDER FROM AMAZON.COM, BN.COM, . . . & OTHER ONLINE OR OFFLINE BOOKSTORES

www.AbleMusePress.com

Sea Level Rising
poems by **John Philip Drury**
978-1-927409-42-8 | Paperback

"Drury's new poems will please many and please often as he celebrates, and with mastery, the inexhaustible waters before and within each of us."
—Dave Smith

"Drury introduces us to a world of love and literature, nostalgia and new experiences—a world where water pervades everything: a constant and comforting reminder that what we depend on is, like us, also always in flux."
—Erica Dawson

"The ever-changing sea defines these poems; Drury explores impermanence—destiny, the future, love, fame, desire—anchored by a rock-solid formal mastery."
—James Cummins

Uncontested Grounds
poems by **William Conelly**
FINALIST- 2013 ABLE MUSE BOOK AWARD

978-1-927409-39-8 | Paperback

"William Conelly . . . has a voice all his own—shrewd, wry, engaging. Even in his more expansive pieces he writes with epigrammatic force."
—Robert B. Shaw

"Conelly commands both strict form and free verse, and his language is often fresh and unexpected. *Uncontested Grounds* will stand as a notable book in this or any year."
—X.J. Kennedy

"[Conelly] is smart and imaginative, and brings a thriving intelligence to life's experiences. I found the poems in *Uncontested Grounds* original, diverse, and lucid."
—William J. Smith

TRANSLATION NOTES

Les Antiquités de Rome (III)

    Nouveau venu, qui cherches Rome en Rome
    Et rien de Rome en Rome n'aperçois,
    Ces vieux palais, ces vieux arcs que tu vois,
    Et ces vieux murs, c'est ce que Rome on nomme.

    Vois quel orgueil, quelle ruine : et comme
    Celle qui mit le monde sous ses lois,
    Pour dompter tout, se dompta quelquefois,
    Et devint proie au temps, qui tout consomme.

    Rome de Rome est le seul monument,
    Et Rome Rome a vaincu seulement.
    Le Tibre seul, qui vers la mer s'enfuit,

    Reste de Rome. Ô mondaine inconstance !
    Ce qui est ferme est par le temps détruit,
    Et ce qui fuit au temps fait résistance.

        — *Joachim du Bellay*
          (Original French version)

NEW FROM

Cup
poems by **Jeredith Merrin**
SPECIAL HONOREE – 2013 ABLE MUSE BOOK AWARD

978-1-927409-34-3 | Paperback

". . . stanzas, rooms, lives./ And you, toiling to make it better,/ whatever your it is./ Each has a cup.

In these forthright and moving poems written in restrained, disciplined stanzas, the stories are told of how we each, "trying to make it better,/ whatever . . . it is," have to find our own cup, and find it acceptable."
—David Ferry

"In *Cup* we meet a poet of rare power and unique originality, unafraid of feeling, able to take on matters of the deepest consequence."
—X.J. Kennedy, Judge for the 2013 Able Muse Book Award

All the Wasted Beauty of the World
poems by **Richard Newman**
FINALIST - 2012 ABLE MUSE BOOK AWARD

978-1-927409-31-2 | Paperback

"*All the Wasted Beauty of the World* is masterful and magnetic . . . Newman's poems, with their formal, lapidary precision, their indelible portraits of life in the cheap bars, back alleys, and rough hewn edges of the Midwest, surprise a hunger in us for a language larger, wilder, and unabashedly loftier than daily speech."
—George Bilgere

"*All the Wasted Beauty of the World* returns us to the real and, consequently, the new by putting on the brakes and asking us to look, if only briefly, beyond our rear-views."
—Dorianne Laux

Details at

ABLE MUSE PRESS

Vellum
poems by **Chelsea Woodard**
FINALIST – 2013 ABLE MUSE BOOK AWARD

978-1-927409-35-0 | Paperback

"The honed music here thus reveals a deeper vulnerability."
—Bruce Bond

"Not the least of the attractions of this gifted young poet's first book is the exquisite, searing precision of her language . . . I predict for Chelsea Woodard a long and enviable career."
—B.H. Fairchild

"In addition to her emotional maturity, part of what makes these poems memorable is Woodard's obvious mastery of language, her flawless sentences."
—Claudia Emerson, from the foreword

Greed: A Confession
poems by **D.R. Goodman**
FINALIST – 2013 ABLE MUSE BOOK AWARD

978-1-927409-38-1 | Paperback

"This poet is alive to everything. You want this book. It's terrific."
—Kelly Cherry

"Goodman is greedy for things of this world—not in the rapacious, bottom-line manner . . . but for the enlightenment of the senses and the enrichment of her poetry. She's sharing the wealth she accumulates."
—John Drury, from the foreword

"Complex yet accessible, these formal and free-verse poems gift us with abundant insights to enjoy."
—Beth Houston

www.AbleMusePress.com

Award Winners from

Corporeality
~ Stories by Hollis Seamon ~
978-1-927409-03-9 | Paperback

- **Gold Medal winner, 2014 Independent Book Publisher Outstanding Book Award**
- **Finalist, 2013 Foreword Review's Best Book of the Year**

"Seamon offers enough thematic and narrative variation to keep each story in this collection fresh." — *Publishers Weekly*

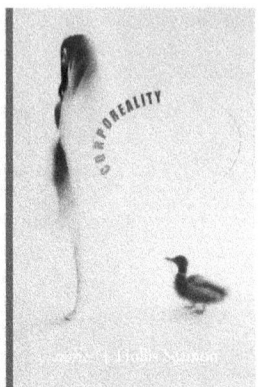

Sailing to Babylon
~ poems by **James Pollock** ~
978-0-9865338-7-7 | Paperback

- **Winner, Outstanding Achievement Award in Poetry from the Wisconsin Library Association**
- **Finalist, 2013 Griffin Poetry Prize**
- **Finalist, 2012 Governor General's Literary Award in Poetry**
- **Honorable Mention, 2012 Posner Poetry Book Award**

"A rich and complex array of subjects and allusions to provide both pleasure and challenge" — *Pleiades: A Journal of New Writing*

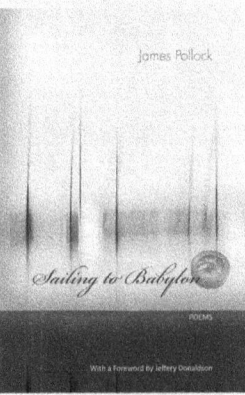

Strange Borderlands
~ Poems by Ben Berman ~
978-1-927409-05-3 | Paperback

- **Winner, 2014 Peace Corps Writers Best Book Award**
- **Finalist, 2014 Massachusetts Book Award**

"This is a must-have book for readers of poetry."
— *Publishers Weekly*, starred review

Life in the Second Circle
~ Poems by Michael Cantor ~
978-0-9878705-5-1 | Paperback

- **Finalist, 2013 Massachusetts Book Award**

"A sensory kaleidoscope where the poems are more like movies."
— Deborah Warren

ABLE MUSE PRESS // www.ablemusepress.com

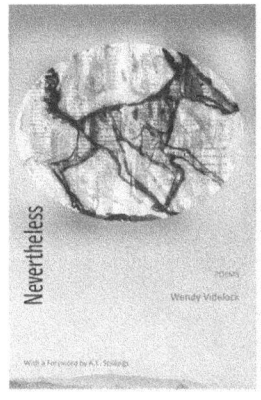

Nevertheless
~ Poems by Wendy Videlock ~
978-0-9865338-4-6 | Paperback

- **Finalist, 2012 Colorado Book Award**

"Videlock is a magician of play and pleasures, wisdom being not the least of these." — A.E. Stallings

A Vertical Mile
~ Poems by Richard Wakefield ~
978-0-9878705-7-5 | Paperback

- **Shortlisted, 2014 Poets Prize**

"Wakefield crafts his verse to exacting standards yet keeps it uncontrived." — David Sanders

The Cosmic Purr
~ Poems by Aaron Poochigian ~
978-0-9878705-2-0 | Paperback

- **Shortlisted, 2014 Poets Prize**

"Aaron Poochigian's technique is masterly . . . and it's easy to be beguiled by these poems' wit and bravura. But the pyrotechnics are used to serious ends." — Dick Davis

Lines of Flight
~ Poems by Catherine Chandler ~
978-0-9865338-3-9 | Paperback

- **Shortlisted, 2013 Poets Prize**

"Lines of Flight is altogether a lively performance." — Richard Wilbur

ABLE MUSE BOOK AWARD WINNERS

Walking in on People
~ poems by **Melissa Balmain** ~

WINNER – 2013 ABLE MUSE BOOK AWARD
SELECTED BY X.J. KENNEDY
978-1-927409-29-9 | Paperback

"Melissa Balmain's poems add to the rhythmic bounce of light verse a darker, more cutting humor. The result is an infectious, often hilarious blend of the sweet and the lethal, the charming and the acidic."
— Billy Collins

Virtue, Big as Sin
~ poems by **Frank Osen** ~

WINNER – 2012 ABLE MUSE BOOK AWARD
SELECTED BY MARY JO SALTER
978-1-927409-16-9 | Paperback

"In his talent for tragedy and comedy, and for mixing them, Osen takes his place in a distinguished line of English-language poets that runs from Chaucer and Shakespeare down to our day."
—Timothy Steele (from the afterword)

Dirge for an Imaginary World
~ poems by **Matthew Buckley Smith** ~

WINNER – 2011 ABLE MUSE BOOK AWARD
SELECTED BY ANDREW HUDGINS
978-0-9878705-0-6 | Paperback

"The range of subjects is equally and as charmingly eclectic, from Neanderthals, Dante, Vermeer, for instance, to College Football Mascots, Highway Mediums, and Spring Ballet Exams. Mental and linguistic agility generously challenge the reader in poem after poem."
— Greg Williamson (from the foreword)

Details at www.AbleMusePress.com

CONTRIBUTOR NOTES

KIM BRIDGFORD is the director of Poetry by the Sea: A Global Conference. As the editor of *Mezzo Cammin,* she founded The Mezzo Cammin Women Poets Timeline Project, which was launched at the National Museum of Women in the Arts in Washington in March 2010, and has since held celebrations at the Pennsylvania Academy for the Fine Arts and at Fordham-Lincoln Center. Her collaborative work with the visual artist Jo Yarrington has been honored with a Ucross Fellowship. Bridgford is the author of nine books of poetry, including the forthcoming *Human Interest.*

CATHARINE SAVAGE BROSMAN is Professor Emerita of French at Tulane University. She was Mellon Professor of Humanities for 1990 and later held the Gore Chair in French. She was also visiting professor for a term at the University of Sheffield. Her scholarly publications comprise eighteen volumes on French literary history and criticism. Her most recent critical volume, *Louisiana Creole Literature: A Historical Study,* appeared in 2013. She has published two collections of personal essays and ten collections of verse, of which the latest is *On the Old Plaza* (2014). New poems and essays are forthcoming in *Measure, Modern Age,* the *San Diego Reader,* and the *South Carolina Review.*

DANIEL BROWN's poems have appeared in *Poetry, Partisan Review, PN Review, Parnassus,* the *New Criterion* and other journals, as well as a number of anthologies including *Poetry 180* (ed. Billy Collins) and *The Swallow Anthology of New American Poets* (ed. David Yezzi). His work has been awarded a Pushcart prize, and his collection *Taking the Occasion* won the New Criterion Poetry Prize. A new collection, *What More?,* was published this year.

DAN CAMPION is the author of *Peter De Vries and Surrealism* and coeditor of *Walt Whitman: The Measure of His Song.* His poems have appeared in *After Hours, Blue Unicorn, Ekphrasis, Light,* the *Midwest Quarterly, Poetry, Rolling Stone, Shenandoah,* and many other magazines, and in anthologies including the recently published *Amethyst and Agate: Poems of Lake Superior.*

BROOKE CLARK edits the epigrams website the *Asses of Parnassus.* His work has appeared in *Arion, Literary Imagination,* the *Rotary Dial, Light, Partisan* and elsewhere.

TERESE COE's poems and translations have appeared in *Threepenny Review, Poetry, New American Writing, Ploughshares, Alaska Quarterly Review,* the *Cincinnati Review,* the *TLS, Poetry Review,*

Agenda, New Walk Magazine, New Writing Scotland, the *Moth,* the *Stinging Fly,* and many other publications, including anthologies. Her poem, "More," was heli-dropped across London in the 2012 London Olympics Rain of Poems, and her new collection of poems, *Shot Silk,* was recently published by Kelsay Books.

MOIRA EGAN's most recent poetry collections are *Botanica Arcana/Strange Botany* (Italic Pequod, 2014*)* and *Hot Flash Sonnets* (Passager Books, 2013). Her poems and essays have appeared in numerous journals in the US, Italy, and elsewhere, and in anthologies including *Best American Poetry 2008, Measure for Measure,* and *The Book of Forms.* In Italy, she and her husband Damiano Abeni have published works in translation by authors including Ashbery, Barth, Bender, Ferlinghetti, Heti, Strand, and Tey. She has held fellowships at the Virginia Center for the Creative Arts (Mid Atlantic Arts Foundation); the St. James Cavalier Centre for Creativity, Malta; the Civitella Ranieri Center, Umbria; the Rockefeller Foundation Bellagio Center; and the James Merrill House, Connecticut.

MAX GUTMANN's plays have been performed in New York City, Orlando, and the San Francisco Bay Area. He has contributed to more than three dozen journals, including *Light Quarterly, Measure,* and *Cricket* for children. His book *There Was a Young Girl from Verona: A Limerick Cycle Based on the Complete Dramatic Works of Shakespeare* sold several copies.

ELISE HEMPEL's poems have appeared in many places over the years, including *Able Muse, Measure, Valparaiso Poetry Review, Poetry,* the *Midwest Quarterly,* and Ted Kooser's *American Life in Poetry.* Her chapbook *Only Child* was published by Finishing Line Press in 2014, and in 2009 she won an Illinois Arts Council Literary Award for a sonnet that appeared in *Spoon River Poetry Review.* She grew up in suburban Chicago and now lives in central Illinois.

BETH HOUSTON has taught writing at ten universities and colleges and has published six poetry books and over three-hundred poems in journals. Way back in 1999, she was *Able Muse*'s first featured poet.

X.J. (real name Joe) KENNEDY professed at Tufts until 1978, when he quit in order to write. His first collection was *Nude Descending a Staircase* (Doubleday, 1961); his latest books are *Fits of Concision: collected poems of six or fewer lines* (Grolier Book Shop, 2014) and a comic novel *A Hoarse Half-human Cheer (*Curtis Brown Unlimited, 2015). Twenty children's books include *Brats, City Kids,* and a novel, *The Owlstone Crown;* among several textbooks is *An Introduction to Poetry,* 13th edition, coauthored with Dana Gioia. A former poetry editor of the *Paris Review,* Kennedy has received the Poets' Prize, the Robert Frost medal of the Poetry Society of America, and the 2015 Jackson Poetry Prize, given by Poets & Writers. He lives in Lexington, Massachusetts, with Dorothy M. Kennedy, coauthor of five books and five children.

STEPHEN KAMPA has two books: *Cracks in the Invisible* (Ohio University Press, 2011) and *Bachelor Pad* (Waywiser, 2014). He currently lives in Florida.

Peter Kline teaches creative writing at Stanford University and the University of San Francisco. A former Wallace Stegner Fellow, he has also received residency fellowships from the Amy Clampitt House and James Merrill House, as well as the Morton Marr Poetry Prize from *Southwest Review*. His poetry has appeared in *Ploughshares, Five Points, Poetry, Tin House,* and many other journals, as well as the *Best New Poets* series and the 2015 Random House anthology *Measure for Measure*. Kline is a founding member of the music/poetry collective Nonstop Beautiful Ladies and director of the San Francisco literary series Bazaar Writers Salon. His first collection of poetry, *Deviants,* was published by SFASU Press in 2013.

Léon Leijdekkers—See page 51.

Amit Majmudar—See page 81.

Autumn Newman is a graduate of the University of Southern Maine's Stonecoast MFA program and has the great fortune of teaching English composition and creative writing at College of San Mateo to amazing, eclectic students. She has published in *Cider Press Review, Suisun Valley Review, and Louis Liard Magazine.* She is currently working on her first book of poems, a (mostly) autobiographical account of domestic violence.

Athar C. Pavis grew up in New York City, attended Mount Holyoke College and studied literature in France. She lives both in Maine and in France where she teaches at the University of Paris. Her poems have been published in the UK *(New Poetry, Candelabrum)* and in magazines in the United States in *Measure,* the *Eclectic Muse,* the *Comstock Review, Slant, Oberon,* the *Raintown Review, Tule Review,* and *Trinacria,* among others. She is currently working on a collection of poetry to be entitled *Pulled Pork*.

Jennifer Reeser is the author of four books of poetry, including *Sonnets from the Dark Lady and Other Poems* (2012) and *The Lalaurie Horror* (2013). X.J. Kennedy wrote that her debut "ought to have been a candidate for a Pulitzer." Her poems and translations of French and Russian literature have appeared in *Poetry, Recours au Poème,* the *National Review,* and anthologies including Everyman's, *Measure for Measure,* Longman's *An Introduction to Poetry,* and *Poets Translate Poets: A Hudson Review Anthology.* Her translations of Anna Akhmatova are authorized by FTM Agency, Moscow. Reeser's own work has been translated into Persian, Czech and Hindi. This sonnet is from her collection, *Indigenous,* forthcoming from Saint James Infirmary Books.

Freeman Rogers lives in the British Virgin Islands, where he is the editor of the *BVI Beacon* newspaper. He is an associate editor of the poetry journal *Smartish Pace,* and his poetry and other writing have appeared in *Slate, Southwest Review, Oxford American, Antioch Review, Measure,* and other publications.

Leslie Schultz studied creative writing at the UW-Madison and at McNeese State University. She now lives in Northfield, Minnesota, where she helped the Arts and Culture Commission establish

Sidewalk Public Poetry in 2011 to publish new work in a truly concrete medium. Her poetry, fiction, and essays have appeared a variety of journals, including *Mezzo Cammin, Swamp Lily Review, Poetic Strokes Anthology, Pacific Review,* the *Northern Review,* the *Madison Review,* the *Mid-American Poetry Review,* the *Midwestern Quarterly, Stone Country, Sun Dog,* the *Wayfarer,* and in a chapbook, *Living Room.* Her book, *Still Life with Poppies: Elegies,* will be published in 2016 by Kelsay Books.

LYNDA SEXSON's work is forthcoming in *Epoch, Fifth Wednesday Journal, Carrier Pigeon,* and *Copper Nickel,* and has appeared in *Black Warrior Review, Fourteen Hills,* the *Gettysburg Review, Ninth Letter, Parcel, New Orleans Review, Image, Kenyon Review,* and others. Her books are *Ordinarily Sacred, Margaret of the Imperfections,* and *Hamlet's Planets.* Her film is *My Book and Heart Shall Never Part.*

ROBERT B. SHAW is the Emily Dickinson Professor of English at Mount Holyoke College. His latest books are *Blank Verse: A Guide to Its History and Use* (Ohio, 2007), which won the Robert Fitzgerald Award, and *Aromatics* (Pinyon, 2011), a collection of poems which was co-winner of The Poets' Prize. *A Late Spring, and After,* his seventh volume of poems, will appear from Pinyon Publishing in 2016.

ANDREA WITZKE SLOT has published a poetry collection, *To Find a New Beauty* (Gold Wake Press), and has completed a novel, *The Cartography of Flesh: In the Silence of Ella Mendelssohn.* Winner of Fiction International's 2015 short fiction contest and finalist in other recent competitions, she explores ways that poetry, fiction, and nonfiction cross boundaries. Her work appears in *Bellevue Literary Review,* the *Adirondack Review, Mid-American Review, Poetry East, Measure, Southeast Review, Nimrod,* the *Chronicle of Higher Education,* and in academic books published by SUNY Press and Palgrave Macmillan. She lives in London and Chicago.

PAUL SOTO lives in Austin, where he studies, writes, and loves. He grew up in Venezuela, San Antonio, and the Rio Grande Valley, and looks to work with children for some time before heading up to graduate school. He is grateful for the support of his loved ones and the inspiration of his heroes, J.D. Salinger, Kendrick Lamar, and Louis C.K. His work has been featured in *Unbroken Journal, Analecta,* the *Nocturnal,* and *Corvus Review.*

DAVID STEPHENSON lives in Detroit, Michigan. His poems have most recently appeared in *Slant, Measure, Angle,* and *Blue Unicorn.* His book, *Rhythm and Blues,* won the Richard Wilbur Award and was published by the University of Evansville Press in 2008.

N.S. THOMPSON lives near Oxford, UK. His most recent book of poetry is *Letter to Auden* (Smokestack, 2010), a verse epistle in rime royal. He is the coeditor with Andy Croft of *A Modern Don Juan: Cantos for These Times by Divers Hands* (Five Leaves, 2014), a collection of new verse narratives bringing Byron's hero into the modern world. His collection *Line Dancing* is forthcoming from Red Squirrel and a collection of his translations of Pier Paolo Pasolini, *Gramsci's Ashes,* is also planned. He is a regular contributor to *Able Muse.*

Jay Udall's work has appeared in publications such as *North American Review, Prairie Schooner, Beloit Poetry Journal, Cimarron Review,* and *Verse Daily.* His latest collection, *The Welcome Table,* was selected for the Mary Burritt Christiansen Poetry Series by University of New Mexico Press, and won the 2009 New Mexico Book Award. He is assistant professor of English and poet-in-residence at Nicholls State University in Thibodaux, Louisiana, where he also serves as chief editor of the online journal *Gris-Gris.*

Wendy Videlock lives on the Western Slope of the Colorado Rockies. Her work has appeared in such outlets as *Poetry, American Life in Poetry, Best American Poetry,* the *Hudson Review,* the *New York Times,* and *Rattle.* Her latest collection is *Slingshots and Love Plums* (Able Muse Press, 2015). Her previous collections are *The Dark Gnu and Other Poems* and *Nevertheless,* also from Able Muse Press.

Jeanne Wagner is the winner of the 2014 Sow's Ear Poetry Review Award and the 2015 Arts & Letters Rumi Award, judged by Stephen Dunn. Her poems have appeared in the *Cincinnati Review, Hayden's Ferry, Alaska Quarterly Review, Shenandoah,* and *American Life in Poetry.* The author of five collections, her most recent book, *In the Body of Our Lives,* was released by Sixteen Rivers press in 2011.

James Matthew Wilson is the author of six books, most recently, *Some Permanent Things* (Wiseblood 2014) and *The Fortunes of Poetry in an Age of Unmaking* (Wiseblood, 2015). A poet, critic, and scholar of philosophical theology and literature, he is Associate Professor of Religion and Literature at Villanova University.

Ryan Wilson was born in Griffin, Georgia. His poems, translations, and criticism appear widely, in journals such as *32 Poems, First Things,* the *Hopkins Review, Iron Horse Literary Review, Measure,* and *Unsplendid,* and he was recently awarded the Walter Sullivan Prize for Promise in Criticism by the *Sewanee Review.* He holds graduate degrees from The Johns Hopkins University and Boston University, and he is currently a doctoral candidate at The Catholic University of America.

Steven Winn is a San Francisco writer whose poems have appeared in the *Antioch Review, Cimarron Review, Poet Lore, Poetry Daily, Prairie Schooner, Southern Poetry Review, Verse Daily, ZYZZYVA* and elsewhere. He has held a Wallace Stegner Fellowship and spent twenty-eight years as an arts critic at the *San Francisco Chronicle.* His memoir, *Come Back, Como* (Harper), has been translated into nine languages.

ABLE MUSE – PRINT EDITION

Able Muse – No. 16, Winter 2013
Jehanne Dubrow, featured poet | **Peter Svensson**, featured artist
978-1-927409-27-5
- with rachel hadas, marly youmans, r.s. gwynn, cheryl diane kidder, a.e. stallings, david mason, chrissy mason, peter byrne, rory waterman, and others

Able Muse – No. 15, Summer 2013
Greg Williamson, featured poet | **Clara Lieu**, featured artist
978-1-927409-21-3
- with dick allen, fred longworth, robert j. levy, haley hach, jonathan danielson, david mason, peter byrne, david caplan, stephen kampa, n.s. thompson, and others

Able Muse – No. 14, Winter 2012
Catherine Tufariello, featured poet | **Nicolas Evariste**, featured artist
978-1-927409-07-7
- with thomas carper, lorna knowles blake, richard wakefield, tony barnstone, len krisak, evelyn somers, gregory dowling, aaron poochigian, and others

Able Muse – No. 13, Summer 2012
Patricia Smith, featured poet | **Andrew Ponomarenko**, featured artist
978-1-927409-01-5
- with wendy videlock, jennifer reeser, richard wakefield, julie bruck, kim bridgford, brian culhane, reginald dwayne betts, and others

Able Muse – No.12, Winter 2011
David Mason, featured poet | **Alper Çukur**, featured artist
978-0-9865338-9-1
- with suzanne j. doyle, timothy murphy, gabriel spera, richard wakefield, lyn lifshin, amit majmudar, rachel bentley, david j. rothman, and others

Able Muse – No. 11, Summer 2011
Catharine Savage Brosman, featured poet | **Emily Leonne Bennett**, featured artist
978-0-9865338-5-3
- with david mason, andrew waterman, john drury, rachel hadas, brian culhane, emily laithauser, leslie monsour, traci chee, and other

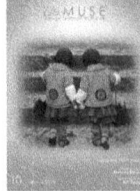
Able Muse – No. 10, Inaugural Print Edition, Winter 2010
R.P. Lister, featured poet | **Massimo Sbrini**, featured artist
978-0-9865338-2-2
- with catherine tufariello, catharine savage brosman, leslie monsour, j. patrick lewis, kim bridgford, nancy lou canyon, john whitworth, peter filkins, and others

Details at www.AbleMuse.com

INDEX

A

"Abbey Light" 53
Able Muse Anthology 139
Able Muse Book Award v, vii, ix, xv, xviii, 119, 122, 123, 126
Able Muse Press vii, 141
Able Muse, Print Edition 132
Able Muse – Print Edition Subscriptions 117
Able Muse – Winter 2012 Print Edition, No. 14 138
Able Muse Write Prize v, viii, 140
Able Muse Write Prize for Fiction 37
Able Muse Write Prize for Poetry 40, 41, 42
"Action Figures" v
"After Reading the News Story of a Woman Who Attempted to Carry Her Dead Baby onto an Airplane" xvii, 37, 39
"A Journey from Which Many Do Not Return" v
All the Wasted Beauty of the World vii, 122
Animal Psalms xvii
"A Photographic Exhibit" 51
"Apology" 6
"A Review of Catherine Breese Davis, On the Life and Work of an American Master" 110
"A Review of David Foster Wallace, *Both Flesh and Not: Essays*" 43
"Artist Statement" 52
Art & Photography 51, 53, 54, 55, 56, 57, 58, 59, 60, 61, 62, 63, 65, 66, 67, 68, 69, 70, 71
Arts & Letters & Love xvii
Asperity Street vi, vii, xv
"At the Base of Quandary Peak" 24
A Vertical Mile vii, 125
"A Wail from the Wild Potato Clan Arbor" 30

B

Bad Fame vii, xiv
Baer, William vi, vii, xv, 127, 141
Balmain, Melissa vii, 119, 126
Bartruff, Jim xvii
Bed of Impatiens xvii
Berman, Ben vii, 124
Book Reviews 43, 110
Boroff, Linda v
Both Flesh and Not: Essays 43
Bridgford, Kim v, 7, 127
Brosman, Catharine Savage v, 102, 127
Brown, Daniel v, 81, 127

C

Campion, Dan v, 18, 127
Campion, Peter v, xvii
Cantor, Michael vii, 124
carmina figurata vii, xvi
"Cathedral Peppersauce" xvii, 42
Cause for Concern vi, vii
Chandler, Catherine vii, 125
Cherry, Kelly 123
"Chronic Pain" 92
"Church Rock, Study #2" 54
Clark, Brooke 19, 127
Coe, Terese 28, 127
Collins, Billy 126
"Commodious Sacrament" 55
Compositions of the Dead Playing Flutes vii
Conelly, William vii, 120
"Connemara" 56
Cooper, James xvii
Corbett, Maryann vii

Corporeality vii, 124
"Correcting Frame" v
Credo for the Checkout Line in Winter vii
Cup vii, 122

D

Danielson, Jonathan vi
Davis, Catherine Breese 110
"Derelict Dream" 57
Dirge for an Imaginary World vii, 126
Dowling, Gregory vi
Drury, John Philip vii, 120, 123
Dybek, Stuart v, viii

E

"Editorial" v
Egan, Moira v, 32, 128
Emerson, Claudia 123
Emmons, Jeanne xvii
Espaillat, Rhina P. xv
Essays 8, 32
Everyone at This Party Has Two Names xvii
"Excerpt from an Intelligence Hearing" 91

F

Fairchild, B.H. 123
"Featured Art" 53
Featured Art 53, 54, 55, 56, 57, 58, 59, 60, 61, 62, 63, 65, 66, 67, 68, 69, 70, 71
Featured Artist 51, 53
Featured Poet 81, 90
Featured Poetry 81, 90, 91, 92, 93, 94, 95
Ferry, David 122
Fiction 37, 73, 96
Finalist, 2012 Colorado Book Award 125
Finalist, 2012 Governor General's Literary Award in Poetry 124
Finalist, 2013 Foreword Review's Best Book of the Year 124
Finalist, 2013 Griffin Poetry Prize 124
Finalist, 2013 Massachusetts Book Award 124
Finalist, 2014 Massachusetts Book Award 124
French 121

G

Goldberg, Midge xvii
Gold Medal winner, 2014 Independent Book Publisher Outstanding Book Award 124
Goodman, D.R. vii, 123
Grasshopper: The Poetry of M A Griffiths vii
Greed: A Confession vii, 123
Griffith, Rob xvii
Griffiths, Margaret Ann vii
Gutmann, Max 4, 128

H

Hartsock, Katie xvii
Heaven from Steam vii
Hempel, Elise v, xvii, 41, 42, 128
Hix, H.L. v, xvii, 42
Hodge, Jan D. vi, vii, xvi
Holding on to the Hard Earth xvii
"Homage to Martin Henson" 58
Honorable Mention, 2012 Posner Poetry Book Award 124
Hooper, Patricia xvii
House Music vii
Houston, Beth v, 107, 108, 128
"How can I" v
Hudgins, Andrew 126

I

"Ice" 107
"In the Crypt #3" 64
"Interviewed by Daniel Brown" 81
Interviews 81

J

Jaggers, Trish Lindsey xvii
Joachim du Bellay 95, 121
"Jockey" xvii
"Journey to No End" 60

K

Kampa, Stephen v, vi, 43, 128
Kareska, Lane v

Kaufman, Ellen vii
Kennedy, X.J. v, 20, 119, 122, 126, 128
Kevorkian, Karen vi
Kim, Eugenia v, xvii, 39
Kline, Peter v, 16, 17, 129
Kreiling, Jean L. xvii

L

Leijdekkers, Léon v, 51, 53, 129
Leithauser, Emily v, xvii
"Les Antiquités de Rome (III)" 121
"Les Braves" 61
Liau, Albert xvii
Life in the Second Circle vii, 124
Light, Carol vii
"Lighthouse" 62
"Lightly Sleeping Are" 21
"L'Île du Guesclin" 59
"Lincoln Barber College" 26
Lindner, April vii
Lines of Flight vii, 125

M

Majmudar, Amit v, 81, 90, 91, 92, 93, 94, 95, 129
"Market Instrument" 28
"Martial's Epigram 2.82" 122
Mason, David 140
McGovern, Martin vii, xiv
McHenry, Eric v
"Meeting David Foster Wallace for the First Time (Again)" 43
Merrin, Jeredith vii, 122
Meyer, Richard vi
"Mirrorform" 16, 17
Modlin, Brad Aaron xvii

N

Nevertheless vii, 125
New and Recent Releases from Able Muse Press vii
Newman, Autumn v, 29, 129
Newman, Richard vii, 122
Nicol, Alfred xvii

"No Future" 90
"Noir" 18

O

"Ode to Silence" 100
"Old Growth" 4
"On Asperity Street" 20
O'Neal, Miriam xvii
"On False Dreams" 19
On the Life and Work of an American Master 110
"On Watching a *Cascade* Commercial" xvii, 40
"Oosterscheldekering, Study #3" 65
Osen, Frank vii, 126

P

Pavis, Athar C. 100, 129
Peacock, Molly xv
"Pentre Ifan, Study #1" 66
Pepple, Alexander v, 139
Poetry 1, 4, 6, 7, 16, 17, 18, 19, 20, 21, 22, 24, 26, 27, 29, 30, 31, 40, 41, 42, 100, 102, 104, 106, 122
Poetry Translation 95, 121, 122
"Polaroid" 73
Pollock, James vii, 124
"Pontigny, l'Abbaye de" 67
Poochigian, Aaron vii, 125
"Protest Poem" 93
Pumpkin Chucking vii
Pushcart Prize, 2016 v

R

Reeser, Jennifer 30, 129
"Risin og Kellingin" 68
Rogers, Freeman 6, 129
"Roman Holiday" 95

S

Sailing to Babylon vii, 124
Salter, Mary Jo 126
"Sanctuary" 69
Scaer, Stephen vii

Schultz, Leslie 1, 129
Sea Level Rising vii, 120
Seamon, Hollis vii, 124
"Sea Wall" 70
"Secluded Confidence" 71
Second Rain xvii
Separate Flights xvii
Sexson, Lynda v, 96, 130
Shaw, Robert B. v, 110, 130
Shipers, Carrie vi, vii
"Shopping with Whitney Houston" v, 29
Shortlisted, 2013 Poets Prize 125
Shortlisted, 2014 Poets Prize 125
Siskel, Callie vi
Slingshots and Love Plums vi, vii, xiv
Slot, Andrea Witzke v, xvii, 37, 39, 130
Smith, Matthew Buckley vii, 126
Smith, Patricia v, viii
Soderling, Janice D. vi
Sorensen, Barbara Ellen vii
Soto, Paul v, 73, 130
Spera, Gabriel xvii
Stallings, A.E. v, ix, 125
Stanton, Maura v
Steele, Timothy 126, 139
Stephenson, David 26, 130
Steyer, Marty xvii
Strange Borderlands vii, 124
Sukach, M.K. xvii

T

Taking Shape vi, vii, xvi
The Borrowed World v, xvii
"The Cloister, One Late Afternoon" 63
The Cosmic Purr vii, 125
"The Curve" 72
The Dark Gnu and Other Poems vii
The Devil in the Milk xvii
"The Fence" 7
The Forming House xvii
"The Ghost Nudges Me to the Cellar" 108
"The Hole in My Shoe" 22
"The Jockey" 41
"The Pianist and the Cicada" 102
"The Purpose of This Object Is Not Certain" 104
"The Strike-Anywhere Match" 94
This Bed Our Bodies Shaped vii
Thomas, Gustavo 140
Thompson, N.S. v, 8, 130
Times Square and Other Stories vi, vii, xv, 141
"Tools of the Trade" 106
Turco, Lewis xv

U

Udall, Jay 106, 131
Uncontested Grounds vii, 120
"Unlocking the Shades in Duddingston Loch: Two Poems by a Contemporary Scottish Poet" 8
Upshaw, Reagan vi

V

"Vamp, Volta, Vows" 32
Vellum vii, 123
Videlock, Wendy v, vi, vii, xiv, 21, 22, 24, 125, 131, 140
Virtue, Big as Sin vii, 126
"Visage" 1

W

Wagner, Jeanne v, xvii, 40, 131
Wakefield, Richard vii, 125
Walking in on People vii, 119, 126
Wallace, David Foster 43
White, Gail vi, vii, xv, 20
"Why Were You Sighing?" 96
Williamson, Greg 126
Wilson, James Matthew 31, 131
Wilson, Ryan v, 131
Winner, 2014 Peace Corps Writers Best Book Award 124
Winner, Outstanding Achievement Award in Poetry from the Wisconsin Library Association 124
Winn, Steven 104, 131

"Woman at Wawasee" 31
Woodard, Chelsea vii, 123
Wright, Rob vi, xvii
Write Prize for Fiction v
Write Prize for Poetry v

X

"Xenia" v

Y

Yezzi, David 119

Able Muse – Summer 2014
Print Edition, No. 17

A TRANSLATION ANTHOLOGY FEATURE ISSUE -
Guest Edited by Charles Martin

WITH NEW TRANSLATIONS BY X.J. Kennedy, Dick Davis, Julie Kane, Willis Barnstone, Tony Barnstone, William Baer, A.E. Stallings, Rachel Hadas, N.S. Thompson, Michael Palma, John Ridland, Jay Hopler, and others . . .

WITH NEW TRANSLATIONS OF Victor Hugo, Arthur Rimbaud, C.P. Cavafy, Catullus, Charles Baudelaire, Francesco Petrarch, Rainer Maria Rilke, Asadullah Khan Ghalib, Horace, Martial, Heinrich Heine, Gaspara Stampa, Dante Alighieri, François Villon, Euripides, Georg Trakl, Paul Valéry, Christine de Pizan, and others . . .

212 pages / $16.95
ISBN 978-1927409-45-9

ORDER NOW FROM ABLE MUSE PRESS AT: WWW.ABLEMUSEPRESS.COM
OR, ORDER FROM AMAZON.COM, BN.COM . . . & OTHER ONLINE OR OFFLINE BOOKSTORES

www.AbleMusePress.com

Able Muse Anthology

978-0-9865338-0-8 • $16.95

Edited by Alexander Pepple • *Foreword by* Timothy Steele

PRAISE FOR THE *ABLE MUSE ANTHOLOGY*:

This book fills an important gap in understanding what is really happening in early twenty-first century American poetry. **–Dana Gioia**

You hold in your hands a remarkable anthology of poems, translations, an interview, essays, short stories and visual art. **–David Mason**

This extraordinarily rich collection of fiction, poetry, essays and art by so many gifted enablers of the Muse is both a present satisfaction and a promise of future performance. **–Charles Martin**

Neither unskilled, lethargic, nor distracted from their proper enterprise, the muses in the past decade have been singularly able, as this outstanding anthology from *Able Muse* demonstrates. **–Catharine Savage Brosman**

Here's a generous serving of the cream of *Able Muse*, including not only formal verse but nonmetrical work that also displays careful craft, memorable fiction (seven remarkable stories), striking artwork and photography, and incisive critical prose. **–X. J. Kennedy**

Mark Jarman, Rachel Hadas, Turner Cassity, Stephen Edgar, Timothy Steele, R. S. Gwynn, Rhina P. Espaillat, A. M. Juster, Geoffrey Brock, Annie Finch, X. J. Kennedy, Timothy Murphy, Jennifer Reeser, Beth Houston, Dick Davis, A. E. Stallings, Richard Moore, Chelsea Rathburn, David Stephenson, Julie Kane, Alan Sullivan, Kim Bridgford, Deborah Warren, Diane Thiel, Richard Wakefield, Rose Kelleher, Leslie Monsour, Lyn Lifshin, Amit Majmudar, Len Krisak, Marilyn L. Taylor, Dolores Hayden, Suzanne J. Doyle, Dennis Must, Thaisa Frank, Nina Schuyler, Misha Gordin, Solitaire Miles, and others.

from **Able Muse Press**

Order or, find more information at: **www.ablemusepress.com**
Or, order at: **Amazon.com, BN.com, . . .**
& other popular online & offline bookstores

www.ingramcontent.com/pod-product-compliance
Lightning Source LLC
Chambersburg PA
CBHW081848170426
43199CB00018B/2852